Field Methods for Academic Research – Interviews, Focus Groups and Questionnaires

in Business and Management Studies

By

Dan Remenyi PhD

Field Methods for Academic Research - Interviews, Focus Groups and Questionnaires in Business and Management Studies
Third Edition

First published March 2011
Second Edition March 2012
Third Edition January 2013

ISBN: 978-1-908272-77-5

Published by: Academic Conferences and Publishing International Limited, Reading, RG4 9AY, United Kingdom,
info@academic-publishing.org

Printed by Ridgeway Press

Available from www.academic-bookshop.com

Contents

How to use this book

This book has been written to help researchers improve their technique with regards interviewing, focus groups and questionnaires.

These techniques are addressed in three separate chapters and thus there is no suggestion that the reader should begin reading this book from the beginning to the end. The three data or evidence collection techniques are addressed from the point of view of having decided to use them through to the point at which the data has been captured and is ready for analysis. There is no discussion of the alternative forms of analysis available.

The forms and letters required to support the research activities described in this book are available on the Academic Publishing website: http://www.academic-publishing.org

Preface

Interviewing, focus groups and questionnaires are often recommended as appropriate methods of data collection for academic research in the business and management field of study. And sometimes this is correct. However research degree candidates are often expected to either know how to use these techniques or they are expected to pick up the knowledge and skills required as they proceed. This is probably due to the fact that every day we see someone being interviewed on television, we hear about focus groups in the news, and we are regularly required to complete questionnaires for all sort of issues.

But academic interviewing is quite different to what is regularly portrayed on television. Academic focus groups are often different to focus groups held for marketing and government surveys and the work required in designing, implementing and managing a questionnaire is really quite complex.

If these three field methods are not planned, implemented and managed correctly they will produce nothing of value and will result in much wasted time for the researcher.

This book looks closely at these three field methods and provides sound advice based on experience on how to work with these data gathering methods.

In addition this book supplies examples of research protocols, letters of introduction, letters of consent and some example questionnaires.

Dan Remenyi PhD
dan.remenyi@gmail.com

Prologue

In its broadest sense the term field methods refers to techniques used for the collection of data outside the confines of a laboratory experiment. The data collection techniques employed and described as field methods varies from one area of study to another. In business and management studies only limited research can be performed in a laboratory setting and thus field methods are important. The three most commonly encountered field methods in business and management studies are interviews, focus groups and questionnaires.

Other field method techniques which are available to researchers in business and management studies include but are not limited to:-

Action Research; Archival Research; Discourse – verbal and written exchanges; Ethnography; Game or Role Playing; Historiography; Journal and Diary Evidence Collection; Observation; Participant-Observer Engagement; Photographic and Video Evidence Collection; Social Network Monitoring; Web Data Collection.

Even a cursory consideration of the above reveals that there is considerable overlap within these field methods and their accompanying research designs. Thus Action Research may involve some discourse recording and subsequent analysis as well as various observation techniques and perhaps extracts from diaries and journals as well as photographic and video evidence.

As a general rule the greater the number of techniques used in the field the greater the likelihood that a rich understanding of the situation will be achieved.

This book restricts itself to issues related to the collection of data or evidence through interviews, focus groups and questionnaires.

Chapter One
Effective interviewing for academic research

The art of conducting effective academic research interviews is not well understood and the practice of interviewing in the field is not always effective. Because nearly everyone has either experienced an interview or watched one on television it is often assumed that there is little to be learnt about an academic research interview. This is not correct. The researcher needs to create an interview protocol and use it as a guide during the interview. The researcher needs to project an empathic but formal image to the informant. A successful academic research interview can be a positive experience for both the researcher and the informant and produce insightful data which may be converted to an interview transcript which is suitable for academic analysis. The academic researcher always needs to be mindful that he or she is a guest of the informant and his or her organisation.

1.1 Introduction

In the context of academic research an interview is a formal technique whereby a researcher solicits verbal evidence or data from a knowledgeable informant. Verbal data or evidence may be obtained in a number of ways besides interviews. Focus groups, conversations, presentations, speeches live and pre-recorded are all potentially useful forms of verbal data. After the verbal evidence has been obtained the researcher will normally need to convert the record of the interview into a written transcript before analysis is performed, and the objective of the interview is to obtain insightful data for this purpose. An academic research interview is unlike any other type of interview such as an employment interview, an appraisal interview or a news broadcast interview. It is especially different to the celebrity interviews which are part of the current television culture. It is sometimes incorrectly thought that interviewing is simple and in fact a natural process, as we constantly see interviews on the television or hear them on the radio (Gubrium & Holstein, 2001). In reality competent academic interviewing is a skill which has to be learnt and improved by practice. The academic researcher will find it challenging to conduct successful interviews and therefore it is important to understand the issues involved and to carefully prepare for an interview (Silverman 1997). The product of an interview may be regarded as interviewer or researcher elicited or provoked data rather than naturally occurring data such as a report from an archive. This distinction needs to be made with care as a report from an archive could itself have been provoked by an incident.

There are several different types of interview and this chapter only addresses semi-structured face-to-face one-to-one interviewing.

Some academics regard an academic research interview as mostly an asymmetrical event where the objective of the researcher is to maximise the amount of data or evidence he/she can collect from the informant and thereby increase his/her likelihood of being able to answer the research question. In this view it needs to be remembered that the objective of the academic research interview is not to have an interesting dialogue with the informant but to collect evidence which will be produced in the form of an interview transcript that will be useful in answering the research question. Other academics are cognisant of the fact that the term interview is composed of the prefix “inter” and the noun “view”. With this in mind it is argued that the researcher and the informant co-create the responses to the questions and thus the data collected is not a simple list of facts. Kvale (1996) points out that there are two philosophical orientations which a researcher may take to interviewing. He refers to these as the miner and the traveller orientations. The miner orientation assumes that the informant is in possession of data or evidence which if it can be extracted by the researcher will lead to answering the research question. This is a distinctly positivist attitude towards research and data in particular. The traveller orientation does not make this assumption. As a traveller the researcher acquires data or evidence which may help directly answer the research question but is equally likely to provide more context and a greater understanding of a wider range of matters of interest. This view which represents an interpretivist orientation is usually seen as providing a wide range of knowledge or understanding.

Before addressing the practical issues related to effective interviewing it is important to mention that the data collected from an interview will at best be the recollections of the informant who may or may not recall the situation being discussed accurately. Some researchers will point out that it is difficult to use the word accurate in this context and they will argue that all memory is subjective and highly influenced by selective perception and selective retention. With this in mind interpretivists will argue that the best which can be obtained from an interview is the recollection of impressions of past event. In addition to this the data is being heard by the researcher who may or may not hear the answers correctly. In addition both the informant and the researcher will have interpreted what has been seen, heard or experienced through their own system of biases. Thus although interviewing is an increasingly important data or evidence collection technique, the data so obtained has to be viewed with caution. It is argued that observation is a better form of data collection than interviewing, but it is not possible to observe past events or for that matter past or current intentions. Where possible however, observation should be used together with interviewing. Wittgenstein (2001) supported this view when he said:-

> *If you want to know whether a man is religious don't ask him, observe him.*

Interviews are always open to the challenge of informant and researcher bias as well as their competence in recalling, recording and understanding the events discussed in the interviews. High quality interviewing is a craft skill which cannot be learnt from books or lectures. Craft skills are only learnt by working alongside an accomplished practitioner. Yet in general universities and business schools do not attempt to create environments in which this skill can be learnt. Researchers are expected to acquire the skills of interviewing through a process of learning by doing with actual informants. This of course leads to the problem that some interviews will not result in valid or reliable data.

Interviewing will not suit all researchers. To be a successful interviewer the researcher needs to be an outgoing and personable individual who can present him/herself in an empathic way. Introverted interviewers will have difficulty with this and would therefore probably be more comfortable using an alternative data collection technique.

1.2 Planning of an interview

Academic research interviews need to be planned if they are to be a success. Not only is it necessary to plan the content of the interview it is also important to plan the number and types of informants required for the study. It is not possible to establish numeric guidelines as to how many interviews should be conducted. Sometimes a small number will be adequate while on other occasions a larger number will be necessary. For an academic research degree it is usual to have a substantial number of informants. There is a theoretical answer to the question of how many interviews should be conducted, which is that interviewing should be continued until data saturation is reached. Data saturation may be defined as the point when additional interviews are not uncovering any new data or evidence. The challenge here is that it is quite subjective to state that no new data is being found and difficult to know how an objective benchmark could be used to justify the claim of data saturation.

With regards who is to be interviewed this chapter focuses on researchers who need to approach individuals and organisations with which they are not employed. Sometimes researchers are able to conduct interviews in-house where they work. In such a case access is often not so difficult and the arrangements to meet the informant may be a little less formal but the other issue discussed here will be relevant.

It can be quite difficult to obtain access to the most appropriate individuals. An introductory letter from the university pointing out that the research is worthwhile can be a distinct help. But often researchers have to compromise and interview those who are prepared to give them time for the interview. The primary issue here is that the researcher should try to reach the most appropriate people and this may take a considerable amount of time and it may be necessary to use indirect routes or indirect approaches such as approaching the gatekeepers. A gatekeeper is an individual or an organisation which can help a researcher obtain access to the right organisations and the most appropriate individuals within them. Gatekeepers may be auditors, consultants, professional institutions, chambers of commerce etc. Within an organisation personal assistants (PA) are often gatekeepers who have been known to jealously guard the time of their bosses and they have been known to simply refuse to pass on requests for interviews. Sometimes the only way of getting around the over protective PA is to accept an interview with another member of the organisation and then, when on the premises, try again to make contact with the intended individual. Sometimes an interview will be offered after business hours. If this is the only opportunity available it sometimes has to be accepted. However it is by no means ideal and should only be used if all other potential opportunities for meeting the informant won't work. Be especially careful of agreeing to an interview over drinks as the informant's attention may not be focused.

The detailed plan for an interview or a series of interviews is referred to as an interview protocol. Exhibit 1.1 at the end of the chapter shows an example of an interview protocol.

In order to be granted an interview the researcher will normally have approached the individual or informant some time in advance. A gatekeeper may have been involved in introducing the researcher to the organisation and to the informant to be interviewed. If a gatekeeper is involved then the researcher should make independent contact, preferably by voice, with the informant before turning up for the interview. Sometimes an informant may ask for a letter from the researcher on a letterhead from the University setting out what is being requested and occasionally a letter from the researcher's supervisor or Head of Department will also be required. An example of such a letter is shown in Exhibit 1.2 at the end of the chapter. Research interviews normally take place on the premises of the informant and this will usually be in his or her office or workstation. Sometimes an informant will suggest that the interview be conducted in a meeting room or even in a refectory or canteen. The researcher may not have any influence over where the interview will take place. It is important to be on time for the interview and researchers will often plan to be at the reception of the organisation some 15 to 30 minutes before the appointed time in order not to be late due to travel delays. If the researcher is early then a period sitting in the reception of the organisation can provide an opportunity for useful observations of the organisation and the people who pass through the reception. Interesting observations made during a waiting period such as this should be recorded and these are referred to as field notes.

What constitutes an interesting observation will differ from situation to situation. Such observations may include noting the parking arrangements, the security procedures in place to handle visitors to the premises of the organisation, dress code, the quality of the reception area and the friendliness of the reception staff. It may also be worth recording if the informant was available on time or whether it was necessary to wait for the informant to be available. Whether refreshments are offered while waiting might also be worthy of note. These minor points may support the researcher in understanding the attitudes which will be obtained from the interview/s. In advance of the visit to the organisation the researcher should have undertaken some research about the nature of the organisation, the types of products and services which it has to offer and acquired some knowledge of the organisation's client base. The more informed the researcher is about the organisation the more likely he or she will obtain more comprehensive information during the interview. If it is a public sector organisation, it is useful if the researcher can obtain information about its stated objectives and its strategy and how these fit into government policy. For both private and public organisations it is helpful if the researcher can obtain information on the dress code and thus dress appropriately. If dress code information is not available then it is better to be slightly more formally dressed rather than being too informal. Part of the interview protocol will address what has to be done during the interview including a script of the main issues to be addressed on arrival and before the researcher leaves the informant.

1.3 Arriving for and starting the interview

On arriving in the office of the informant, it is important to establish a warm but formal rapport by perhaps shaking hands and thanking him or her for giving you their time for the interview. This gratitude should be genuine and sincere. It is important that you explain the purpose of the visit and that you reiterate the topic of your research and also the specific research question. Some researchers suggest that the informant should spend a few minutes talking about themselves and providing information about their academic and professional background. Having a short 12 line bio at hand could be useful in this situation. Any questions asked by the informant about the researcher's background should be answered openly.

It is then essential to enquire if the informant is still prepared to proceed with the interview. It is useful to specify how long you think the interview will last. One hour is a satisfactory period of time in which a considerable amount of data can be collected and the duration will not be too tiring for either the researcher or the informant. It is also important that the informant has the knowledge to answer the type of questions which will be asked of him/her. If the person turns out not to be a knowledgeable informant then point out that a misunderstanding has occurred and see if he/she can point you to an appropriate person. Assuming that he/she is knowledgeable and agreeable and the time period is satisfactory, the next step is to complete the requirements of the university's ethics committee.

This involves handing the informant a Research Participants Information Document which spells out what the research is about and how the evidence/data will be used. An example of a Research Participants Information Document is supplied in Exhibit 1.3. Allow five minutes for this document to be read and answer any questions which are raised. Then offer the informant a copy of a Letter of Consent to sign. Make it especially clear that anything said will be held in total confidence by the researcher. An example of such a document is provided in Exhibit 1.4.

With regards seating during the interview, if possible try to avoid sitting directly opposite the informant, across a desk, but rather be seated at adjacent sides of a board room table. If there is the opportunity to sit in some comfortable chairs this can be advantageous. But in practice the researcher often has no option other than to accept the seating arrangement offered by the informant.

Ensure that the researcher's mobile telephone is switched off.

1.4 How to capture the data

The objective of the interview is to acquire data or evidence which will be used to help answer the research question. As this data will be verbal the researcher needs to capture it as quickly as possible. Interview notes are always essential (unless one has a remarkable memory) and these will normally be scribbled as the informant is speaking. However when taking down such notes, even if the researcher is skilled in shorthand techniques, it is difficult and will often lead to incompleteness. There is also the problem with scribbled notes that sometimes the researcher won't be able to read his or her handwriting later. It is therefore helpful if the researcher is able to record the interview on a non-intrusive device. This is clearly a significant advantage to the researcher as having such a recording will greatly facilitate the subsequent creation of a transcript of the interview. The researcher needs to have had the ethics committee specific approval for this and also the informant has to have agreed to the recording. Obtaining such permission from either the ethics committee or the informant can be a problem because of the need for confidentiality. The textual transcript of an interview can be easily anonymised whereas a voice recording cannot be. Permission to record will not always be given by either the ethics committee or the informant[1].

When recording an interview, the informant may ask to have the recorder switched off while discussing a sensitive question or issue. Such a request should be complied with. If a recording device is used then voice levels should be tested before the interview commences. It is useful to make it clear to the informant that their voice recording will only be held until the research has been completed.

Some researchers have taken an assistant with them to interviews where the assistant has been responsible for the recording of the interview leaving the researcher to focus on the discourse with the informant.

1.5 The interview schedule

To an important extent the effectiveness of the interview depends on the questions, listed in the interview schedule, which the researcher will put to the informant. Thus the directness of the questions, the exact wording and the order in which they are put, are all critical issues. In addition the questions asked need to be focused on the research question and its sub-questions. This alignment between the research question and the interview schedule is of considerable importance and thus time needs to be spent by the researcher reflecting on what questions to ask and how these questions may be put to the informant. Leading questions should be avoided and the researcher needs to be careful of the tone with

---

[1] Some researchers argue that the recording of the interview introduced a bias to the interview. Some people are fundamentally introverted or shy and will thus be uncomfortable in having their voice recorded. Despite this they will give permission for the recording to be used as they will not feel that they can refuse the request to record. If the informant is uncomfortable it is unlikely that the researcher will obtain full or comprehensive answers to questions. Other informants who are more extraverted may enjoy be recorded and they may possibly supply extra unwanted commentary.

which the questions are asked. Direct questions can be problematic and sometimes an indirect question can produce much better results. An example of this could be, if the researcher asks the informant; "Are you involved in the strategic policy formulation process?" and the informant is not, this could lead to the informant feeling that he or she is somehow not as senior in the organisation as they should be. This could generate some embarrassment and discomfort between the informant and the researcher. If the question is asked, "Could you please tell which members of staff are involved in the strategic policy formulation process?" then if the informant is a member he or she will say so, but there can be no suggestion that the researcher thought that the informant should have been in this type of position and thus no embarrassment. The researcher has to ensure that he or she does not appear to the informant to be directly or indirectly judgemental (Silverman 2000).

With regards to the wording of questions, it is critical that the researcher and the informant share a common vocabulary or professional language[2]. If the researcher asks a question and the informant does not understand the words used then the outcome of the interview will be of little or no use. Sometimes it is suggested that the researcher should provide a glossary of terms for the informant. It is also suggested that the researcher could prepare diagrams which could be used to explain the processes about which the researcher wants to enquire. Glossaries and diagrams can be helpful in some circumstances. If the researcher is collecting data about how the informant sees the organisation fitting into a taxonomy or how it's policies might be categorised in terms of some theory then a list of options within the taxonomy will be useful and a diagram of the elements of the theory will help the informant provide useful information.

---

[2] Sometimes the informant and the researcher will have slightly different definitions of a concept and when this occurs the differences should be highlighted and reconciled if possible (Silverman 2001).

But such props have to be used with care. Sometimes such documents are indicative of possible misunderstandings between the researcher and the informant and if they are used then the researcher will need to exercise considerable caution when reflecting on and analysing the resultant transcript.

On commencing the interview the researcher should have in his or her possession an interview schedule. An example of an interview schedule used by a student is shown in Exhibit 1.5. This document has two parts. The first part of this document referred to as descriptive questions is used to record some basic information about the organisation and the place of the informant in it. These descriptive questions should be kept to a minimum and any question which the informant might consider, under normal circumstances, as personal should be avoided. Thus do not ask for a person's age or income or race unless such issues are central to the research.

The second part of the interview schedule contains the detailed individual questions which are intended to facilitate the answering of the main research question i.e. a list of the issues about which the researcher wishes to obtain data. Once again parsimony is required and it is important that this list should not be a lengthy one of "wouldn't it be nice to know" type questions.

In interview situations the questions need to be highly focused. Normally six to eight questions or topics should be the limit for a one hour interview. The researcher may offer this list to the informant to give him/her a feel for what the researcher wants to achieve during the interview. It is important to note that interviews lend themselves to the acquisition of non-technical and non-numerical data. If technical data is required then the researcher can ask the informant if he/she can supply some documents covering this point.

It is not unusual for a research project, especially at doctoral level, to require 25 interviews or perhaps even more. In fact a quick inspection of doctoral dissertations in university libraries will reveal work which has included 50 to 100 interviews, although current research usually does not require this many. One of the important advantages of interview research is that the researcher is learning about the research question as he or she moves from informant to informant. This means that the researcher often wants to fine tune the interview schedule as the research progresses. It is also the case that the researcher will improve his or her interview technique and this may result in other changes to the interview schedule. Thus, the interview schedule with which the interviews commence may well be different to the interview schedule with which the research is concluded. This should not produce any material problems in the subsequent analysis of the data.

In preparing the questions for the interview schedule the researcher needs to bear in mind that he or she is looking for insights which could shed light on a new way of understudying the situation being researched. This means that the questions asked need to penetrate beneath the obvious routine of the situation to look for this new understanding. It is challenging to find such questions and the researcher needs to persist with this if a suitable result is to be achieved.

1.6 The interview

Before asking any of the questions in the interview schedule it is important to situate the informant in the company structure by enquiring to whom he or she reports and also establishing who reports to him or her. This information will be useful during the analysis of the data. There is also some boilerplate questions concerning the name of the informant and the length of service in the organisation. It is usually thought that a relatively general question should be asked at the start of the interview. This could be used to make the situation more relaxed. However it is generally not possible for research interviews to be particularly relaxed as both the researcher and the informant usually have to work hard at understanding each other during the interview. In addition it is important to get to the point of the interview as soon as possible. From the researcher's point of view he/she has to ensure that the informant understands the questions asked. If the informant does not understand the question then points of clarification need to be made. The researcher needs to take copious notes and to watch the progress of the recording if that is also being taken. The types of questions normally asked by academic researchers will be challenging and the informant will often have to reflect, perhaps deeply on the subject matter. The researcher may need to be patient (Richie and Lewis 2003). Listening skills are required by the researcher who needs to pick up nuances, such as variations in tone, intensity and rhythm (Scheurich 1995), as well as straightforward data. There is a separate body of literature which addresses the subject of positive or active listening skills and researchers who intend to use interviewing as a data collection technique should have consulted this literature. The researcher will also have to remain aware of the body language of the informant which often indicates much about the person and his/her attitude to the research project. All these different types of data i.e. the direct verbal evidence, the body language of the informant and any other reports which the informant may produce, need to be incorporated into the final interview transcript produced with the raw material obtained during the interview.

If the informant does not give what the researcher feels are complete answers to the questions in the interview schedule then he/she may ask the informant for further details. It is suggested in the literature on academic research interviews that the researcher can probe the informant and indeed this can sometimes be the case. However just as often, if the informant does not answer the question fully, it is an indication that he/she does not want to answer that question. Under such circumstances probing could be inappropriate. It is important for the researcher to always bear in mind that they are a guest of the informant and his/her organisation and that the highest standard of politeness has to be maintained. Therefore only the gentlest probing should be undertaken.

Prompting is another issue which is similar to probing in that it occurs either when the informant does not respond to a question at all or when the informant replies with an answer which indicated that he or she has not understood the question. The problem with prompting is that it is possible that by prompting the researcher is actually encouraging a particular answer i.e. is "putting words into the mouth" of the informant. Thus if prompting is used it has to be done with considerable care. Some researchers would be strongly opposed to allowing any prompting to take place during an interview.

A form of prompting is to show the informant a diagram which indicates the relationship between the issues being discussed or perhaps to have written definitions of concepts with which the informant might not be fully conversant. Here the objection raised is that if the informant needs such prompting then perhaps he or she was not an appropriate person to involve with the research.

Sometimes the researcher may fall behind schedule due to being unable to control long answers supplied by the informant. In such a case do not speed up the questioning process but rather ask the informant for a few more minutes of his/her time so that you can complete the interview schedule. If on the other hand the interview questions are finished early then the researcher may use that time to try to obtain additional insights concerning the organisation. However it is important that the informant does not feel that the researcher is just engaging in time killing or idle gossip.

Because of the concentration required in listening to the replies the interview is a very tiring process and the researcher should feel able to pause occasionally to catch up with his/her notes or to simply catch his/her breath. Sometimes too much detail is supplied by the informant and the researcher may have to politely say that he/she is only interested in a high level reply to the question. The interview time is precious and therefore needs to be conserved for the main questions. The 80/20 rule applies in this situation and it is important that the researcher keeps focused on the main data items of interest.

Sometimes there can be a high level of interruptions due to the informant not having cleared the interview time of routine work matters. This can produce inadequate answers to the questions being asked. If the researcher feels that this is happening it is better for the researcher to ask if the interview could be rescheduled to a more suitable time.

It is not a trivial matter to prepare a competent interview schedule which should have been pre-tested and field tested in advance. Both these tests are required so that the researcher can be confident that the questions listed on the interview schedule are intelligible. The pre-test is often conducted with friends and colleagues and is designed to identify the more significant mistakes and ambiguities. The field test needs to be conducted using individuals who are similar to those who will eventually be interviewed. These testing procedures are important because the researcher can become so close to his or her work that they cannot see the potential problems with their questions.

Sometimes the field test shows that the interview schedule was adequate and required very little if any change. In such cases the researcher may include transcripts of these field test interviews in the body of his/her research. If material changes are made to the interview schedule then the data acquired during the field test interviews need to be omitted from the transcripts.

1.6.1 The end of the interview

The interview should end with the researcher once again thanking the informant for the time provided and the opportunity of discussing the issues related to the research question. The researcher should restate the questions addressed in the interview and give a brief synopsis of the data supplied by the informant. This is regarded as an important debriefing aspect of the interview. If the informant does not feel that his or her input has been correctly represented by this summary the researcher should immediately take note of the changes required.

The researcher should offer the informant a summary of the findings of the research and if he/she does not already have the e-mail address of the informant that may be requested. Another request which may be made at this stage is for the informant to suggest other members of the organisation who might be helpful to the researcher in obtaining more data. The researcher may even ask the informant to suggest other organisations which may be approached in pursuance of the objectives of the research. Sometimes the informant will actually introduce the researcher to another informant. This technique of seeking new informants at the end of the interview is referred to as snowball sampling.

As the researcher is leaving the office of the informant it is useful for the researcher to ask permission to be allowed to contact the informant again if, when the interview record is transcribed, there is the need for some points of clarification. It might also be appropriate to send a letter/email of thanks to the informant. An example is shown in Exhibit 1.6

1.7 Field notes

Soon after the completion of the interview the researcher should record his/her impressions of the informant and the environment in which he or she works. This is one of the main uses of field notes. Field notes may be recorded at any time and they certainly assist the researcher in recalling impressions which were not part of the formal interview. An example of a form to use for field notes can be seen in Exhibit 2.7.

Commenting on the attitude displayed by the informant to the organisation and to the researcher is a common use of field notes. Such a comment can be useful when analysing the transcript especially if a form of hermeneutics is used. However it needs to be mentioned that the researcher should not read too much into how he or she has been greeted by the informant as it may be artificial due to the novelty of the informant being consulted by a researcher. Being consulted by a researcher can be regarded as an indication of importance in the organisation.

Another important use of a field note is to record issues which have not been addressed in the detail required by the researcher. Thus the field note is where matters to be followed up may be recorded[3].

Some researchers argue that taking an occasional field note is not adequate for senior academic research and that a Field/Research Diary should become an integral part of the research progress. Such a diary would be updated after each interview as well as being updated perhaps each week. It would be unrealistic to expect an academic researcher to update such a record each day, although some fastidious researchers might.

1.8 Photographs

As most mobile telephones now have an integrated camera, and most researchers will have a mobile telephone in their possession, it is sometimes useful to take photos of the premises as well as individuals working there. In a sense such photographs play a role similar to field notes as they will facilitate the researcher's recall of the context and the circumstances in which the interviews took place. Photographs should not be taken without the explicit approval of the organisation and also the approval of the individuals involved. If it is the researcher's intention to take photographs then this should be stated in the ethics protocol and have received authorisation from the ethics committee.

The requirement to take photographs needs to be specifically mentioned in the Letter of Informed Consent or if the intention is to take a large number of photographs perhaps the issues should be raised in a separate Letter of Consent.

1.9 Interview assistants

Sometimes it is not possible for the researcher to conduct all the interviews himself or herself. In such cases the researcher, if he or

---

[3] Miles and Huberman (1994) suggests that the researcher should create a contact summary form immediately after the interview using the data captured and the field note as the first step in developing an interview transcript.

she has sufficient funds, may obtain assistance from other appropriate researchers. For data collected by others the researcher has to ensure that only capable and responsible people are chosen. These people need to be carefully briefed before they carry out an interview and they need to be debriefed afterwards. The researcher needs to check the quality of the transcripts which are produced by such people and be confident that their work has been performed diligently. There should not be any compromise with regards the quality of the data produced by these helpers.

1.10 The impromptu interview

An issue which is seldom raised in the literature is that of the impromptu interview. And impromptu interview is not a formal data collection activity but rather a brief conversational exchange between the researcher and an informant. This exchange will be less structured than a research interview and will almost certainly be of a shorter duration. This phenomenon will occur under several different circumstances. The first of these is when the researcher is well known to the organisation in which he or she is researching. In such a case the researcher may be involved in some activity like action research or perhaps participant observer research. The impromptu interview could occur at any time such as when the researcher encounters an informant in the canteen, at the water cooler or simply in a passage way. The second way in which an impromptu interview can arise is when the researcher is waiting for his or her appointed time to interview the informant. Sometimes when seated outside the informant's office other members of staff will commence a conversation with the researcher. Data supplied in this way can be useful and should not be ignored[4]. A third way in which such an interview could take place is when the researcher encounters an informant who had been interviewed sometime before. The

[4] Some researchers argue that impromptu interviews will suffer from a self selection bias and therefore should be avoided. In the sense that all informants need to provide the researcher with permission to conduct the interview there is invariably some level of self selection present in this process.

informant might point out to the researcher that further to the interview he or she has something else to add. When this happens the informant's remarks can be insightful. The researcher needs to confirm that the informant is prepared to have such informal remarks included or added to the transcript.

However these impromptu interviews are problematical in a number of different senses. The first issue is that it is unlikely that the researcher will have an appropriate informant information document and Letter of Consent ready to be signed by the unscheduled informant. Even if the researcher had copies of these documents on his or her person the production of them could easily stifle the spontaneous conversation which the researcher is about to have with the informant. Secondly these impromptu interviews are likely to be quite short and thus they will not be structured in an easy way for the purposes of comparison with the other interviews. In most cases it is better to create a detailed field note in which these impromptu encounters are recorded. Of course in the case where an informant wishes to elaborate on his or her previously held interview then the new data is simply added to the transcript for analysis in the usual way.

1.11 Unexpected challenges

Not all interviews proceed as smoothly as described above. Sometimes the researcher is misdirected to someone who does not actually have the required data or evidence. If this is the case the researcher should not spend time idly chatting, but rather politely close the interview and proceed to the next research activity. Sometimes the informant has been instructed by a senior manager to make him/herself available and they do not wish to so do. Some people simply do not enjoy being interviewed. In such a case the researcher will normally have to accept this as a wrong turn and move on. A researcher should not try to force answers from someone who is reluctant to offer their opinions or knowledge. The literature on interviewing speaks of probing when in the opinion of the researcher an adequate answer is not given and probing may be used if the researcher feels that the original question was not fully understood. Occasionally informants can be negative about the research and this should not influence the researcher. When an informant is unpleasant about his/her organisation the researcher should be careful about how this could be reported. If the informant uses unacceptable language the researcher needs to report this in the transcript without repeating the particular words[5]. No expletives should ever appear in an academic transcript.

There may also be occasions when the informant may make inappropriate comments concerning race and gender and this can result in the researcher feeling uncomfortable. It is important that the researcher should not engage the informant in an argument. If the comments are truly offensive the researcher should simply bow out of the interview as gracefully as possible. Having any sort of argument with an informant is counterproductive and may lead to the researcher loosing access, not only to that particular informant but to the informant's whole organisation.

Another possible challenge is that a despite being generally well disposed towards the researcher an informant may refuse to sign the Letter of Consent. Such a refusal to sign presents a problem. As the Letter of Consent is designed to protect both the informant and the researcher this is unusual, but when it does occurs the researcher needs to act with considerable caution. Different universities will have different policies towards this situation and it is useful for the researcher to have discussed this with his or her supervisor in advance. It would not be appropriate for the researcher to refuse to interview the informant but the researcher could treat the data collected under these circumstances differently and perhaps not include it in the transcript.

---

[5] It may be advisable for the researcher to inform his or her supervisor if this happens as dealing with an unsuitable informant may have consequences further down the research process.

1.12 Advantage: semi-structured interviews

There are important advantages which semi-structured interviews have over questionnaires. As the researcher proceeds from one interview to another he or she will hopefully be learning how to improve their interviewing technique which will help in obtaining richer data from subsequent informants. The researcher will also be able to fine tune the questions themselves. This is obviously not available to a mass data collection technique such as when a large scale survey using questionnaires is employed. Also the researcher may become more sensitised to the environments in which the interviews are taking place and therefore be able to produce more comprehensive field notes leading to a fuller understanding of the situations being studied.

On leaving an interview it is important for the researcher to make a field note concerning how well he or she feels the interview has proceeded and if there have been any lessons learnt about matters that should be avoided or for that matter included in the next interviews. If the interview was successful the researcher should note which lessons can be used next time around. A note should be made if there were issues which the informant was unable to answer and thought given to who might be better able to supply relevant data in this regard.

1.13 The interview alone

It is important for the researcher to appreciate that interviewing informants without collecting other sources of evidence is unlikely to provide a sufficiently comprehensive understanding for the purposes of a research degree. Thus the researcher needs to collect reports, financial accounts, publicity material, photographs and any other documentary evidence which is available during or after the interview.

The items mentioned above may be provided by the informant or the organisation from their own records and thus this is referred to as internal data. In addition the researcher may wish to collect external data from customers/clients, newspapers and journals, investment analysts, chambers of commerce and other interested bodies.

1.14 Interview success

There is no simple answer to the question as to whether the interview was a success. Any answer depends on where the researcher is in his or her research journey. It depends upon, amongst other things, whether the research is exploratory, descriptive or formal. Success will also depend upon the degree to which the researcher feels confident about the integrity of the information supplied by the informant. The following are some specific issues which need to be explicitly considered when attempting to answer the question of the evaluation of an interview. There are five possible dimensions to an interview which may directly relate to its success or lack thereof. These are:-

- Was the data obtained in line with the expectations of the researcher?
- Was an appropriate amount of relevant data collected?
- Did the interview reveal new issues or dimensions which shed new light on the research question and its possible answers?
- Did the interview support the researcher's current understanding of the topic and the theory behind it that is being researched/studied?
- Was the informant able to facilitate the findings of another appropriate informant?

With regards to the amount of data collected it is clear that if the informant has little or no knowledge of the subject which the researcher wanted to discuss then the interview would probably not be successful. But the amount of relevant data alone does not indicate success. Researchers are normally looking for something else as well as simple information. They are mostly looking for new or original insights into how individuals or organisations responded to procedures or policy changes or other interventions into the usual working of the organisation. Academic researchers are always looking to get below the surface of what appears to be happening to the organisation from the point of view of the casual observer. It only by understanding what is happening at this level that it is possible to make a contribution to the body of theoretical knowledge.

In creating research questions the researcher invariably has some expectations as to the type of answer which can be expected. If the answers to the questions were substantially out of line with what the researcher expected then the interview may not have achieved its objectives. However the fact that all the answers were according to expectations may not be all that useful either. Many researchers would argue that if an interview reveals new issues or dimensions which shed new light on the research question and its possible answers, then they have achieved a high level benefit from the interview.

The researcher will find that with some experience they will be able to sense if the interview is going well and be able to make an assessment of whether their time with the informant has been well spent.

1.15 Telephone, video and internet interviewing

It may be difficult to obtain an appointment to see the individual who might have the required knowledge to assist in helping answering the research question. When this occurs then a telephone interview may be the only way of obtaining access to that individual. Telephone interviews are not considered ideal as the researcher does not have the opportunity of obtaining the additional information resulting from visiting the organisation and seeing other members of staff on their premises.

Information and communications technology has added a new dimension to interviewing opportunities. The availability of inexpensive teleconferencing technology allows electronic face-to-face interviewing to take place. This is certainly an improvement on telephone interviewing, but it is not as effective as interviewing in person. There are now numerous video conferencing products available for use on personal computers and lap top computers, many of which are free. The use of this technology certainly makes access to certain individuals easier than it was before.

Researchers will have an exchange of e-mails with an informant and this will be referred to as "e-mail interviewing". Although data or evidence obtained in this way may be useful, it would not be reasonable to call this process interviewing. There are occasions when e-mails could become an important adjunct to an interview. If the transcript of an interview is sent to an informant and this leads to additional comments being made in one or more e-mail exchanges then it would be acceptable to include these e-mails with the original transcript.

1.16 Group interviewing

There can be an opportunity to interview more than one informant at once. This might occur when the researcher is collecting data from a number of individuals who perform a similar function. For example it might be useful to interview two salesmen about sales management issues in their organisation. It could also occur that the researcher might interview an executive and his or her personal assistant. Interviewing more than one person at a time is difficult and even more care needs to be taken to ensure that the data is correctly recorded. Interviewing more than 2 or 3 informants at one time can be too difficult to obtain reliable data.

A group interview will always introduce an element of bias. In such a situation Informants cannot help but hear each other's replies to the questions and this will have an effect on what they tell the informant. If the informants in the group interview have different statuses in the organisation the more junior members will almost inevitably defer to the more senior members of the group. Thus if group interviews cannot be avoided then considerable care needs to be taken by the researcher to identify such biases and he or she will have to take action to try to minimise these. Perhaps it might be possible to re-engage the more junior or introverted members of the group again at a different time.

The term group interviewing is sometimes incorrectly used to describe focus groups. A focus group is a small number of individuals, say four to six, who are brought together to discuss a subject in the presence of the researcher. The researcher acts as a facilitator for the discussion but does not contribute to it. A transcript of the discussion is developed and used as data in the same way as the transcript of an interview.

1.17 Interviewing in a different language

Some researchers wish to collect evidence from individuals who speak a different language. In these cases an interpreter may be used. However it has to be appreciated that it is difficult to find interpreters who can operate at the level required for this type of work. Simply being bilingual will often not be adequate to capture the meaning of the questions put and the answers offered. Thus it is quite probable that the researcher will not be able to acquire as thorough an understanding of the transcript as he or she would have obtained if the interview had been conducted in the researcher's mother tongue. It has been suggested that one way of ensuring the faithfulness of the translation is the translate-retranslate procedure which requires the translation from English to the different language to be retranslated back again into the English. This is a well established approach when questionnaires are involved and a similar type of technique could be used when it comes to interview schedules. But the problem which arises is a cultural one. Sometimes the concepts in which the researcher is interested do not exist in the same way in the other culture and thus no direct translation is possible. In such cases a language-cultural translation is required and when dealing with an interview it is difficult to ensure the authenticity of this type of exchange of ideas.

Working across languages and cultures is always difficult and the cost of translation and the use of interpreters can often be high and the processes involved with the translation will slow down the research. For most academic purposes working across languages and cultures is an unwelcome complication which should only be undertaken with considerable care.

1.18 Protection of informants and its limitation

The pledge of informant confidentiality is a particularly important issue. The purpose of the confidentially requirement is to ensure that no harm may come to the informant as a result of participating in the research. The anonymisation of the transcripts and the promise of ensuring that the data is held securely until it is destroyed are all part of the professional handling of the relationship between the researcher and the informant. Even if the researcher encounters what might appear to be questionable business practice confidentiality should be maintained[6].

There are occasions when it may be impossible to ensure anonymity. If for example a large, important, high visibility, organisation is included in the researcher's sample, the discussion of the organisation and/or the context in which it operates may well be enough to disclose which organisation it is and even who is speaking. If the informant begins to make personal and/or inappropriate remarks the researcher may suggest that he will not include these in the interview transcript to ensure that they are not traced back to the informant.

However there are two circumstances in which the researcher is under a legal obligation to report what is seen or heard. If there is any evidence of the individual or the organisation being involved in any terrorist activity or if there is any evidence of money laundering this has to be reported to the police.

---

[6] Researchers argue that the question of reporting behaviour which they find objectionable should be a matter of personal conscience. An example is the presence of bullying in the organisation. It is hard to disagree with the proposition that something should be done about such a situation, but it may well be that reporting this is the last action a researcher undertakes in the organisation. It is generally agreed that no one likes a whistle blower.

There is a problem of defining what might be regarded as evidence of involvement in terrorist or money laundering activities. Most researchers will not be able to make a decision in this respect and will need to take legal advice. Furthermore it is obvious that reporting such activities would terminate the researcher-informant relationship.

1.19 Non-disclosure agreements

Some organisations believe that an undertaking of maintaining confidentiality is not enough and that a non-disclosure agreement be signed by the researcher. A non-disclosure agreement has more legal weight than a confidentiality clause. Many researchers will not have a problem with signing such an agreement as it is not the objective of academic research to abuse the trade secrets of the informant or his or her organisation.

In some cases the informant requests that the supervisor also sign the non-disclosure agreement. The logic of this is clearly that what the researcher knows about the organisation will be conveyed to the supervisor in some way during the research. However informants do not always appreciate that the researcher will present his or her data and findings at colloquia during the period of the degree. Nonetheless, if the supervisor's signature on a non-disclosure agreement is required and if the researcher wishes to retain the informant then it is probable that the signature will be given.

The final issue in relation to non-disclosure agreements is that some informants will cooperate with the researcher provided that the information supplied by them is not published and sometimes this can mean that the data supplied cannot be included in the dissertation. This condition is normally unacceptable in the academic environment. Some universities will allow the student to apply for a delay in publishing the dissertation or allowing it to be made available in the university library. This is sometimes referred to as putting an embargo on the dissertation. To achieve this, the researcher usually has to apply to the university authorities who will require a substantial reason before allowing this to happen. Most universities are publically funded and as such the knowledge created therein should be available in the public domain. The length of an embargo is often 12 months although sometime 24 months can be obtained.

f such an embargo is not accepted by the researcher then there will be no option but to exclude that informant from the research.

1.20 The transcript

The purpose of the interview is to acquire data from which a transcript will be produced. The transcript is not an end in itself but is rather the data required for the analytical part of the research. The transcript will normally be produced in two steps. Firstly a transcript will be produced for each interview. The "raw" material used here will be the notes taken by the researcher, field notes written up and sounds from a voice (on rare occasions a video may be used) recording. The other important ingredient which is used here is the memory of the researcher. As memory is an important ingredient it is crucial that the transcript be written up soon after the interview. Secondly when all the interviewing is complete for the organisation being studied, each individual transcript is drawn together into a document which represents the total data obtained through the interviewing process for that part of the research. As mentioned before, 20 interviews would not be uncommon in a case study environment and thus the researcher may be working with as much as 200 or more pages of transcript.

Normally the transcript of a one hour interview could be as short as 3 typed pages and as long as 15 pages. The number of pages will depend on how much data has been collected and the richness of the environment in which the interview took place. If the interview was held in an organisation's head office there could be much to be said about how that appears to function. Similar data could be acquired from an interview on a factory floor.

Writing a transcript is a challenging task. The researcher needs to be aware of his or her biases and prejudices and these should not influence how the researcher reports the interview and the premises in which the interview took place. An unbiased account can be hard to produce and one of the few things that can be done to minimise bias is to read the notes and listen to the recording of the interview a number of times. During this process the researcher needs to be as reflective as possible and to challenge himself or herself as to the most appropriate way to record what has been said and what has been meant by the informer, bearing in mind that these may be different.

Transcript writing is a time consuming business as it is more than simply committing to paper or to a computer screen the words of the informant. Firstly there is often an amount of work associated with the disposing of extraneous words such as "umm" and "ah". The transcript is written up without using any expletives which may have been used by the informant. However blank spaces may be left in the transcript where unacceptable language was used. Secondly where ambiguities arise the researcher has to describe these and to suggest what he or she believes is the most likely meaning of these words. The writing up of a transcript, even a relatively short one, is a multi- hour activity.

Even where the research is funded and thus there is money for the transcriptions of audio tapes, the researcher still needs to closely edit this type of transcript as the typist may not have understood what the voices were actually saying on the tape recording or they may have interpreted what was said incorrectly.

1.20.1 Verifying the interview transcript

When the transcript has been fully written up it is sometimes thought to be appropriate that the informant read it so as to verify that the researcher has correctly understood the data which was supplied. This may be the last step in the preparation of the transcript before the researcher starts his/her analysis of the data received. Sometimes this is a relatively straight forward matter where the informant reads the transcript document and either states that it is a fair reflection of what was said or perhaps asks for a few small amendments to be made in order to improve the understanding of the situation. However sometimes complications occur and the informant may wish to consult his or her superior. In one recent incident the researcher was told that he would have to wait for the corporate lawyers to look over the transcript before proceeding with the analysis. Unfortunately the corporate lawyers took 12 weeks to reply to this matter. On receiving a copy of the interview transcript informants have been known to require considerable changes when they see what they have said in black and white. Sometimes they regret having revealed information which a third party might consider inappropriate. On one recent occasion the informant told the researcher that he had changed his mind completely and no longer wanted to be part of the research. This is of course allowed and it is spelled out in the Letter of Consent that the informant may withdraw at any time. However such an event is unfortunate and counterproductive to the research process and may set the work back considerably. Some academics would argue that it is not necessary to send the transcript for verification and if this is the case then proceeding without this review may be acceptable.

1.21 Traps to avoid

Researchers should not expect informants to behave as though they are in a confessional. Informants will often omit to disclose information which could make them look less than professional. They can also simply forget inconvenient facts. Informants will sometimes gossip about their colleagues in a non-flattering way and researchers should be aware that such information should be confirmed if it is to be used. The issue of lying is addressed below.

Each interview should be written up as soon as possible. It is important to create the transcript when memories of the interview and the researcher's reactions are fresh in the mind. Trying to remember exactly what was said and by whom after 3 or 4 interviews can produce problems. This is especially true if the interview was not recorded and if only incomplete field notes are available.

Not every interview will be a success. Many academic research interviews are actually poor. This is primarily because researchers are insufficiently prepared for them. Also universities generally do not provide adequate training in this skill.

From a practical perspective a mistake that researchers are inclined to make is not to introduce themselves properly and not to convince the informant that the research will be useful to him or her or to his or her organisation. Ideally the topic of the research should be of immediate concern to the informant and there should be some obvious value in the findings.

It is easy for the researcher to lose control of the interview and then the informant may wander off the point. This can lead to two difficulties which are that time is wasted and the researcher may become bored. The pace of the interview is always important. As mentioned above sometimes the informant may take more time to answer questions than the researcher has planned. In cases where the time allocated to the interview runs out, do not attempt to make up time by rushing through questions. The only reasonable step to take is to ask for a second interview. If this is refused then ask for the interview period to be extended. It is important that the researcher does not give the impression that he or she thinks this is the fault of the informant.

Although it is normally accepted that informants do not deliberately lie, it is unrealistic not to think that informants will have personal agendas. This does not mean that the researcher should be sceptical of anything he or she is told. However it is important not to take all the data at face value. It is important to verify what you are being told. This may be done through the process of triangulation. This requires the researcher to speak to multiple informants and to also obtain multiple sources of data or evidence such as corporate reports and documents. Triangulation provides a much richer understanding of what is actually happening in the organisation and therefore leaves the researcher in a better position to evaluate what he or she is being told. Photographs of the organisation and the employees can be of use in this respect.

In some situations it is relatively easy to put words into the mouth of the informant. This should be avoided. The questions should not be "leading questions" nor should they indicate the values of the researcher. It is important to remember the existence of the confirmation bias i.e. the researcher has a built in tendency to interpret what he or she is hearing in such a way that it will confirm their own beliefs. In addition the informant may want to give the researcher the type of answer that the researcher wants to hear.

Sometimes the informant will offer a large number or facts and figures as well as diagrams and charts and this can consume a significant part of the time allocated to the interview. If the informant starts to search for these then it is acceptable for the researcher to ask him or her to compile these papers after the interview.

It is not an easy task to find suitable informants and researchers are sometimes tempted to use friends or family as informants. While such people may be helpful during the pretesting of the interview schedule they should not be used as proper informants as they will tend to have a bias, probably towards answering the question in the way they think the researcher wants to hear[7]. Many researchers do not obtain access to the informants they would really like to interview and thus compromises may well have to be made. Nonetheless there are often a number of people besides the most senior executives in an organisation who can provide the data required.

Occasionally an informant will ask the researcher "To whom have you already spoken?" Sometimes this question is asked entirely innocently but on other occasions the informant is trying to find out what types of opinions the researcher has already received. When this question is asked the researcher should politely decline to answer it, saying "Not only is the content of the interviews confiden-

---

[7] An examiner of a research degree would be very critical of any research which has been based on interviews of friends of the research. It is also important for the researcher not to use colleagues unless there is a special reason for this such as when action research is being perused. Action research implies that data will be obtained from or derived from the opinions of colleagues.

tial but the names of the individuals are also confidential". This should not give any offence.

1.22 Reflections on interviewing

Before concluding a chapter on interviewing it is appropriate to reflect on the assumptions and the values which drive the use of interviewing in academic research and also to recall the objective of academic research. But first it is important to note that there are different points of view as to what constitutes reflective thought. Dewey (1991) defined reflective thought in the following way:-

> *Active, persistent, and careful consideration of any belief or supposed form of knowledge in the light of the grounds that support it, and the further conclusions to which it tends, constitutes reflective thought.*

This definition addresses the main aspects of reflective thought but it overstates the extent of which it is required. The researcher needs to balance the amount of energy spent on current research activities with the energy required to make sure that what he or she is doing will lead to the result required.

The objective of academic research is for the researcher to produce some new understanding (or knowledge) which contributes to the established body of theoretical knowledge. In very broad terms, this is achieved by having an appropriate research question and by knowing what type of data is required to answer the question. To use interviewing as a data collection tool the researcher needs to believe that appropriate data can be gathered through the processes of questioning and recording answers from individuals who have made themselves available to the researcher. Why should this be the case? It has been argued that data/evidence supplied by informants is less convincing than data/evidence acquired by the direct observation of the event or situation being studied (Silverman 1997). This may be the case but researchers often want to explore past events and also researchers may wish to explore situations to which they will not be given direct access such as meetings of the board of directors. Similarly, with courts of law there is often no choice but to accept historic data/evidence, which may also be referred to as testimony, after the event, from relevant informants. In any event it has been shown even by experiment that eye witness data can be misleading. There is no such thing as a fully objective-independent observer. Everyone has a series of biases or prejudices with which they observe the world. The fact that both the informant and the researcher are endowed with these does not make research impossible but rather more challenging. If the researcher has reflected on this and come to the interview aware of the biases or prejudices which may be present, a better result will often be obtained in that a more nuanced account of what has been said will be produced.

Within the assumptions underpinning the validity of the interview there are two other important issues which are Is the informant able to understand the questions which are put to him or her? and Is the researcher able to understand and use the data so obtained?

With regards to the issue of whether the informant is able to understand the questions there are challenges in ensuring that this is the case. In the first instance there are different degrees of understanding and it is possible that the researcher and the informant may be working at different levels. Sometimes this situation will be reflected in answers that the researcher feels are too simple or answers that he or she cannot understand. In these cases the questions may be put again during the interview. If this does not produce a seemingly more satisfactory result the researcher and informant may explore the issue further. Paulos (1998) suggests that understanding comes from what he calls a "talk Tango" where the participants need to take a number of steps to conclude what they mean. But sometimes the differences in understanding may not be so apparent. The questions put to informants are often trying to elicit data about aspects of processes which are not necessarily obvious without reflection. Reflection takes time and this implies that interviewing should not be rushed and that both researcher and informant need to be wordsmiths i.e. to be skilled at choosing the right words to explain their meaning. This is not trivial and researchers, let alone informants, often fall short of this requirement. It is sometimes possible to see when the researcher and informant have not achieved an appropriate level of mutual understanding when the transcript of the interview does not offer any insights into possible answers to the research questions.

The second issue is *how can the researcher use the data provided by the interview to facilitate the answering of the research question*? There is, of course, no short answer to this question. In academic research questions may be answered by a theoretic approach which uses logic and reference to authority or by empirical data.

In this chapter we are concerned with empirical research and thus our interest is focused on data. From an empirical point of view to answer the question above an understanding of data is needed. A high level synopsis of the concept of data could be:-

Research questions are answered by identifying appropriate data and by examining it in a way which is conducive to understanding what that data is able to tell us. Data takes many forms and can be usefully described as anything which stimulates one or more of the researcher's five senses in such a way that he or she believes that it can make a contribution to answering the research question.

In practice data is generally seen as either numeric or quantitative or composed of non-numeric or qualitative information. These two categories are often seen, incorrectly as being exclusive i.e. quantitative data is composed of only numbers and qualitative data has no numbers included. In fact the situation is more complex with tables of figures and graphs thereof being included in qualitative data. On the other hand what is considered quantitative data may have been originally captured in the form of words which have subsequently had values attached to them.

Interviews are essentially a qualitative data gathering tools. In some circumstances qualitative data may present the optimal way of finding an answer to the research question. During an interview there may well be some numeric data offered by the informant as well as the verbal answering of questions. It is appropriate to collect this numeric data as it is often seen as strengthening and providing completeness to the qualitative data obtained from the interviews.

The outcome of an interview should not be considered raw data in the same way as the data collected during an experiment of from a questionnaire might be. It is naive to think that the research does not have a direct effect on the answers proffered by the informant. How this may be handled is the theme of another book.

1.23 Conclusions and summary

The interview is an increasingly popular way of collecting data or evidence in the social sciences and it has a role to play in both qualitative and quantitative research. An interview may be a very positive experience where the researcher and the informant may engage in a two way conversation about the topics in the interview schedule. Such a two way conversation may enrich the experience of the interview for both the researcher and the informant. This is sometimes likened to a dialectic experience. On such occasions useful data frequently results. Of course it is important that the conversation between the researcher and the informant does not wander towards issues which are not directly related to the research i.e. the interview schedule. It is essential to bear in mind that the objective of the interview is to obtain insightful data which will be used in creating a transcript which will in turn facilitate the answering of the research question. For this reason considerable time should be allocated to the preparation of the interview schedule. Only questions which have a direct bearing on how to answer the research questions should be included.

It is critical not to confuse academic research interviews with any other type of interview. They are quite different. An academic research interview is part of a process which has always to be carefully planned and the researcher should comply closely with the interview protocol. Interviewing and especially academic interviewing is not a natural skill. It has to be learnt and practised. Likewise, listening with the attention required for academic research is not a trivial task and researchers should ensure that they have a high degree of skill in this respect.

The relationship between the researcher and the informant is a core issue. This relationship often depends to a major extent on maintaining confidentiality of what is said. As mentioned above this can be a difficult issue. However the researcher will seldom publish the whole transcript in the dissertation or the published paper and thus to a considerable extent the identity of the informant will be protected. Confidentiality should only be deliberately broken where it is clearly required by the law. If this type of situation arises then the researcher should take legal advice.

Not all interviews will be successful. Sometimes the apparent informant is the wrong person who has little to offer the researcher. On occasions the informant has been instructed to see the researcher but does not feel that the research is worthy and that this exercise is of no value to him or her or his or her organisation. Then there is the informant who does not have enough experience of the subject of the research question to be able to supply any data that is likely to lead to any new insights. If such a person is encountered the researcher should politely terminate the interview and look for someone with more to offer.

Impromptu interviews may take place at any time and researchers should be prepared to handle these on virtually no notice. Notes may be taken on the basis of field notes which can be incorporated into the transcript in due course. The camera of a mobile or cell phone can be a helpful way of recording information to subsequently incorporate into the transcript.

Researchers often like to present the transcript of the interview and the field notes to the informant for verification. This is good practice and some researchers feel that it is an important aspect of due diligence on the part of the researcher. If this is done then there may be delays and other problems regarding the content of the transcript may arise.

It is important to always remember that in most environments an academic researcher is the guest of the informant and the informant's organisation and that any unfortunate impoliteness will reflect badly on him/her and his/her Institution. If the researcher is not getting the information required from the knowledge informant he/she needs to find another knowledgeable informant who will be prepared to talk openly.

Finally sometimes quantitative researchers say that using interviews as a research tactic is only for those who want to minimise the work of finding hard data, as well as for those who are frightened of statistics. Both of these suggestions are nonsense. Interviewing is not an easy option. In fact it is hard work often taking more time and effort than collecting numeric data. Furthermore the analysis of interviews is every bit as challenging as any numerical analysis.

1.24 End note

To conclude here are the 10 principles for making interviews work for academic research:

1. Carefully plan all aspects of the interviews using the interview protocol provided at the end of this Chapter.
2. Make sure that whoever is interviewed is knowledgeable about the topic and that the data obtained from him or her will help answer the research question.
3. Be careful of interviewing more than one person at a time as these situations are difficult to manage and may result in data which is not especially useful.
4. Appear knowledgeable and be open with the informant during the interview.
5. Ensure that the ethics protocol is complied with and ensure that permission is obtained to record and perhaps photograph the informant and his or her office etc.
6. Learn the skills of active listening.

7. Keep the timing that has been agreed in advance. Only stay longer at the specific invitation of the informant.
8. Thank the informant and ask for permission to telephone him or her with points of clarification later.
9. Create field notes or make entries in a field diary as soon as possible after the interview.
10. Produce the interview transcript as soon as possible after the interview.

Exhibits for Chapter One

Exhibit 1.1: Interview Protocol

Item No	Issue	Detail	Notes
1	Research Topic	How IT investment benefits are evaluated	
2	Research question	How to develop the theory of ICT investment analysis so as to incorporate intangible benefits and soft costs	
3	Informant/s	Joe Smith Financial Director XYZ Ltd e-mail joe.smith@xyz.com	
4	Location	Head Office, Central London	
5	Gatekeeper	Yes. Tom Jones tom.jones@aaa.com	
6	XYZ Ltd	Any special issues about XYZ Ltd that has been in the media recently	
7	Arrival at premises	Arrive early, look for additional data by inspecting the building and watching staff, and make field notes	
8	Pre-interview	Thank informant, restate research topic and research question, mention gatekeeper if relevant, check informant is knowledgeable and prepared to offer his knowledge and views, recording permission and equipment, present ethics issues and letter of consent	
9	Interview schedule	Interview schedule presented to informant – copy attached	
10	Interview	Approximately 50 minutes of careful questions and answers	
11	Post-interview	Thank informant, ask for other contacts if required, ask for permission to ask points of clarification	
12	Other data	Have any reports been offered by the informant? If so collect them	
13	Reflection	Make post interview field notes	
14	Transcript	Compile all the data obtained and begin production of transcript	

Exhibit 1.2: Letter of Introduction

University Name

University Address

Date

Informant Name

Address

Dear Mr/Ms J Bloggs

This letter serves to introduce Mr/Ms XXXXXXX who is a researcher in my Department at this University.

Mr/Ms WWWWW is currently researching in the field of XXXXX. His/her research question is YYYYY. He/She believes that interviewing you on your organisation's views on this topic will be of considerable value to his/her research.

This research project will lead to a better understanding of ZZZZZ which will be of use to managers and executives in organisations such as yours.

I would be most grateful if you would be so kind as to give him/her any assistance which you can.

Yours sincerely,

Head of Department

Exhibit 1.3: Research Participants' Information Document

The purpose of this document is to explain to potential research participants the nature of the research which is proposed and the role which he or she is being invited to play in that research.

	Issue	Example Detail
1	Name of Researcher Contact Details If part-time state employers name and address	Tom Jones e-mail address and telephone numbers The XYZ Consulting firm[8].
2	Title of Research Project	Development of a good practice framework for *creating* a structured test procedure within small to medium sized companies
3	Purpose of the Study	The purpose of this research is to develop a framework identifying the steps which a small to medium sized organisation may undertake to develop a test team structure
4	Description of the Study	The research will take the form of a questionnaire and interviews.
5	Duration of the Study	12 months
6	What is involved and how long will it take?	Contributors will be asked to complete a short questionnaire and partake in an interview. You will be asked if you are prepared to have a voice recording of the interview and you may decline to so do. The time required is estimated to be approximately 60 minutes.
7	Why you have been asked to participate?	You have been asked to partake in this study due to your experience with testing techniques and having worked in an environment where testing is conducted.

---

[8] It is possible that there could be a conflict of interests between a part-time researcher's interests as an academic researcher and his or her employment position. A recent example was when a part-time masters student while working for an accounting practice wished to research accounting firms' practices with regard to expert systems. When he was asked to explain how other accounting firms would speak to him about their use of expert systems he declared his intention to state that he was a masters degree candidate and to omit the fact that he was an employee of a competitor. This was unacceptable and the part-time student had to find another topic and other informants to approach.

	Issue	Example Detail
8	What will happen to the information which will be given for the study?	The information will be held in a confidential manner while the work is being collated. Notes, transcripts and tapes (if any) will be kept under lock and key. Following the successful completion of the research all material collected as a result of the questionnaire and interviews will be shredded and/or destroyed.
9	What will be done with the Results of the Study?	The results of the questionnaire and interviews will be reported in the findings section of the research work. This will be done in a completely anonymous manner.
10	What are the possible disadvantages?	There are no costs to you associated with your involvement with this study. It is not envisaged that any negative consequences will accrue to you from your contributors in this research.
11	In what way will the study be beneficial and to whom?	It is hoped that this study will provide a useful framework to small and medium sized companies embarking on a software implementation project where they will have to invest significant resources in the test phase. The framework will detail various options available to the management in establishing a test team.
12	Who has reviewed this Study to ensure that it complies with all the requirements and ethical standards of the university?	The Ethics Committee of the School of Big Black Boxes at the Unitary College Dublin have approved this research proposal and granted permission for the research to commence/continue.
13	Can permission be withdrawn having previously been granted?	Yes, all contributors shall retain the right to have their contributions to the research withdrawn at any time. In addition the contributor has the right to refuse to answer any question asked during the interview. They may also ask to end the interview at any time.
14	Can you refuse to answer any question?	Yes. The contributor has the right to refuse to answer any question on either the questionnaire or in any part of the interview.

Exhibit 1.4: Letter of Informed Consent

I, Jane Doe, agree voluntarily to take part in the research project being conducted by John Brown as part of the requirements for his Doctorate/Masters Degree or Research paper at UCD. I have read the Research Participants' Information Document and I understand the contents thereof. Any questions which I have asked have been answered to my satisfaction.

I understand that the information which I will supply is confidential and that it will be anonymised and will only be used in the findings of the research.

I understand that I do not have to answer all the questions which may be put to me. The information which I provide will be held securely until the research has been completed (published) after which it will be destroyed.

The information which I provide will not be used for any other purpose.

I understand that I am entitled to ask for a de-briefing session or a copy of the research at the end of the project.

I have been informed that I may withdraw from this study at any time and that any information which I have supplied will not be used for this research and any records held relating to my contribution will be destroyed.

Signed ....

Date ....

Exhibit 1.5: An example interview schedule

Before the interview begins record the name of the informant, the date and the time at which the interview is commencing. Also record the title of the informant and note his or her position in the organisation.

Research question

To what extent do female entrepreneurs experience more difficulties growing their businesses than do their male counterparts? If it is correct that female entrepreneurs experience more difficulties then what sort of advice can be given to women who wish to grow their businesses?

Target informants

This interview schedule will be used to interview women entrepreneurs who have been in business on their own or in partnership for a minimum of two years.

Duration

It is expected that the required data/evidence will be collected within 50 minutes.

Descriptive questions

Name of organisation ....

Department or division............................

Name of informant Given Name.................

Family Name...................

No of year's service with the organisation............

Research questions

1. Can you briefly describe your business for me?
2. By how much has your business grown since its inception?
3. How would you like your business to grow in the future e.g. new products / new markets and what do you consider are the greatest challenges you face in growing your business.
4. On a scale of 1 to 10 please indicate how difficult you think it will be to raise funds for:-.

5. New products
6. New people
7. New ideas
8. New premises
9. Please indicate why you think you will have problems in raising funds for such projects.
10. Is your business capital intensive? How have you raised funds for your business in the past? What problems have you had in raising funds? Describe the sources of funding you would use to grow your business in the future?
11. On a scale of 1 to 10 please indicate how difficult you think it will be to raise these funds.
12. What would determine when you would stop growing your business?
13. What demands (financial, personal, time wise, family, partner, etc.) will business growth place on you as an owner of the business and what factors do you consider in determining whether or not your business is successful?
14. Are there any other issues which I have not raised but which are relevant to my research question on which you would like to make a comment?

Exhibit 1.6: A letter of thanks

University Name

University Address

Date

Informant Name

Address

Dear Mr/Ms J Bloggs

Thank you for the opportunity of having discussed issues related to my research question. Your input into this has been very helpful.

If you wish I would be pleased to send you an electronic copy of my dissertation or perhaps the section of my work where my findings are listed. Please let me know what you would prefer.

Yours sincerely,

Researcher

References

Dewey J, (1991), *How we think*, Prometheus Books, p6, NY

Gubrium J & Holstein, (2001), *Handbook of Interview Research Context and Method*, (2001) ISBN 0761919511

Kvale S, (1996), InterViews: An Introduction to Qualitative Research Interviewing, Sage, London

Miles M and M Huberman, (1994), Qualitative Data Analysis, Sage, Thousand Oakes, Ca

Paulos J A, (1998), *Once upon a number*, Allen Lane, London

Richie J and J Lewis, eds., (2003), *Qualitative Research Practice, A guide for Social Science Students and researchers*, Sage, London

Rubin H and I Rubin, (2005), *Qualitative Interviewing, 2nd Ed*, Sage Publications Inc, Thousand Oaks, Ca.

Silverman D, (1997), *Interpreting Qualitative Data: Methods for Analyzing Talk, Text and Interaction*, Sage, London

Silverman D, (2000), *Doing Qualitative Research A Practical Handbook*, Sage, London

Silverman D, (2001), *Interpreting Qualitative Data Methods for Analysing Talk, Text and Interaction*, Sage, London

Scheurich J, (1995) "A postmodern critique of research interviewing", *Qualitative Studies in Education*, Vol. 8, No 3 p239-252.

Wittgenstein L, cited in Edmond D and J Eidinow, (2001) *Wittgenstein's Poker*, p7, Faber and Faber, London

Useful websites

http://www.edu.plymouth.ac.uk/resined/interviews/inthome.htm#4

http://regionalworkbench.org/sequence_09-07/files/ppt/www-public-asu-edu-kroel_interviews.pdf

http://www.public.asu.edu/~ifmls/artinculturalcontextsfolder/qualintermeth.html

http://www.ehow.com/way_5234507_qualitative-interviewing-techniques.html

http://www.inside-installations.org/OCMT/mydocs/Microsoft%20Word%20-%20Booksummary_Interviews_SMAK_2.pdf

http://www.socialresearchmethods.net/kb/intrview.php

http://managementhelp.org/evaluatn/intrview.htm

http://www.leeds.ac.uk/educol/documents/000001172.htm

http://www.youtube.com/watch?v=7AxNI3PhvBo&feature=related

Chapter Two
Focus groups for academic research

Focus groups are frequently discussed as part of an academic research programme but they are often misunderstood by both research degree candidates and their supervisors. The primary function of a focus group is to allow researchers to listen to and observe conversations between knowledgeable informants. It is a non-quantitative research technique. The purpose of the technique is to obtain access to established knowledge in order to clarify issues for the researcher. The output from a focus group should not be considered as a main source of data in a research project but rather as supporting data. A focus group is normally most useful at the outset of the research where it is necessary to clarify issues related to the suitability of the research question and at the end of the research when the application of the findings becomes important. A focus group uses a number of knowledgeable informants with different views about which they will debate and this debate should lead to revised or new ideas for the researcher. It is not the intention to obtain any degree of consensus from a focus group. A focus group is facilitated or moderated by an experienced researcher and after the focus group a transcript is created from notes taken and from the recording of the event. Field notes may also be used to record the tone of voice, the sitting posture and the dress of the participants. There are a number of important ethical issues related to focus groups and these are addressed. Focus group work is intensive and the facilitator will usually need an assistant. This paper offers guidance as to how to set up and manage a focus group. It also discusses the creation of the transcript resulting from the focus group and how to decide if the focus group has been successful.

2.1 Introduction

There is very little common agreement regarding the proper use of focus groups in academic research (Barbour 2007). Some researchers see them as a type of multiple concurrent interviews while others regard them as having little to do with interviewing. In this paper focus groups will be defined as qualitative evidence collection opportunities which involve a facilitator or moderator leading a discussion or conversation between a number of knowledgeable informants on a topic which will facilitate the development of the understanding required to answer a research question. In academic research focus groups are not simple data collection exercises but rather a technique for bringing together experienced individuals who through an open but focused dialogue can assist in clarifying issues for the researcher.

Focus groups have been frequently used in market research to collect data concerning products, advertising, price setting, quality issues and other marketing decisions[9]. They have also been used extensively in government policy decision making. In the academic environment focus groups are used to improve the researchers understanding of more demanding issues than those described above. Focus groups are complex events which need careful management. They have become a useful technique with which academic researchers need to become familiar.

The academic focus group brings together a number of suitable knowledgeable informants of similar status[10] and invites them to participate in an open discussion on a subject which will provide insights into possible answers to the research question. The members of the group should not normally be previously acquainted with each other and this is seen as a way of accessing a range of different opinions. Focus groups need to be convened in a friendly

---

[9] Marketing focus groups are often invited to spend an hour talking with each other about a product or service and then offered a gift voucher or some of their organisation's products or services as a reward for making the time available. It is unusual for an academic focus group to offer such an incentive.

[10] The issue of similar status is that a focus group which includes senior people and junior people may not work well as the junior members may not feel comfortable in airing their views in front of the senior members.

non-threatening environment where the participants can discuss the research in an open way.

The objective of such a group is to provide verbal data or evidence spoken in the "own words" of the informant. The evidence may be captured by note taking during the group discussion and this may be supported by voice or video recording or both. It is often said that the main difference between a multiple interview and a focus group is that in the focus group informants are expected to state their opinions and argue for them as well as asking each other questions to challenge other informants' opinions and in so doing to solicit clearer explanations of the matter being discussed. The facilitator plays a relatively passive role[11] whereby he or she will set some questions and allow the discussion to move, largely, at its own pace[12].

A focus group is said to be focused in two respects. In the first place the group is focused in terms of the subject and questions which are put to the group. Secondly the group is focused in respect of the individuals who have been invited to participate in the deliberations. Some researchers have suggested that bringing people together as a group will sometimes allow them to speak more freely about the subject than if they were being interviewed on a one-to-one basis. A group dynamic will often emerge and this will draw individuals out to give more comprehensive views and opinions and this is in itself more data. Although this may be so in many or most cases in other instances the group dynamic may work in the opposite direction, especially if the discussion becomes dominated by a small number of people.

---

[11] If too passive a role is played by the facilitator then the conversation can wallow in the shallows of gossipy exchanges and not make adequate progress to understanding the issues involved.

[12] It has sometimes been said that the focus group is similar to a Knowledge Cafe. However this is a misunderstanding as the function of a Knowledge Cafe is to allow the participants to become familiar with each other's thinking and thus promote a greater understanding within the group. It is not the intention of focus groups to do this.

Some researchers argue that focus groups are not intended to be used to either collect or discuss technical or quantitative data, but they may be used to explore attitudes, opinions and beliefs concerning technical or quantitative data. According to Krueger (1994):

> *It is important to keep in mind that the intent of focus groups is not to infer but to understand*

This view of Krueger is not without its critics as it appears to some researchers to be far too limiting. But in the sense that inferences from data require thorough examination and considerable reflection, he is technically correct.

There is no suggestion with a focus group that the members should try to find consensus or even some common ground and agree on the issues being discussed. In fact if all the members of the focus group were in agreement then the focus group would probably be of reduced value.

Researchers should not rely on focus groups as the sole source or even an important source of data for a research project. Other sources are essential as part of a suitable range of data and to triangulate what we have heard from focus groups. Triangulation is not so much needed to verify the data obtained from the focus group but rather to obtain a richer understanding of the situation being studied.

To use focus groups successfully a researcher needs to be both an outgoing person who can feel comfortable managing the discussion among a number of people as well as a talented organiser who can make all the arrangements required to bring together 6 to 8 people for such a discussion.[13]

---

[13] It might be possible to outsource the task of facilitating the focus group but it would always be much more satisfactory for the researcher to undertake this task him or herself. If the facilitation of the discussion is handled by someone else then the researcher should at least be present through the duration of the focus group

2.2 Theoretical underpinning

The theoretical underpinning of focus groups is that individuals can, through the process of conversation, explore attitudes, opinions and beliefs to a greater extent than simply stating them to a researcher. Specifically the focus groups are intended to reveal through conversation[14] between the participants a deeper understanding of their experience, attitudes and beliefs. In a conversation one idea expressed often triggers other ideas and much of the value of the focus group lies in the chain of such ideas. The intention is that conversation or debate allows experiences and attitudes to be better understood for what they are. The conversation is regarded as having a synergetic affect. It is important to note that the conversations which take place are not between the researcher and the focus group members but rather the conversation between the focus group members. It is assumed that the conversation or debate between these individuals will create a dynamic which will cause them to reflect on their ideas as they speak and thus lead to more interesting insights on the topic being researched.

The members of the focus group need to be expert or at least knowledgeable about the subject related to the research question which is being discussed[15]. Therefore focus group members need to be carefully selected. In market research focus group members are sometimes selected randomly from such environments as people moving through a railway station or sitting in a waiting room in a hospital. This is not appropriate for an academic focus group where the members have to be carefully chosen. The members of a focus

---

meeting. It is possible that outsourcing the facilitation could impinge on the validity of the research.

[14] The term conversation is used here to encompass a range of different type of verbal exchanges including, discussion, dialogue, discourse and argument.

[15] In market research focus groups are sometimes established comprising of individuals who know nothing or very little about the questions being posed. This is not usual in academic research. Academic research generally relies on working with knowledgeable informants, although clearly there may be exceptions to this from time to time.

group may be seen as a purposeful sample[16] of knowledgeable individuals who normally do not know each other.

The insights obtained from a focus group can be very useful to the researcher in several different contexts which are discussed below.

2.3 When to use focus groups

Focus groups are not suitable for general evidence collection in academic research, i.e. focus groups should not be used as the primary form of data collection, but rather as an ancillary technique which is appropriate in a number of specific instances[17]. The most frequently encountered uses of focus groups in academic research are:-

- Obtaining general contextual background to the research question
- Generating testable propositions or hypotheses
- Eliciting issues and factors around a specific domain or topic
- Field testing or piloting a measuring instrument
- Interpreting the findings of the research

It is not intended that the above is an exhaustive list of focus group uses but rather examples of the most frequent uses to which focus groups are put.

2.4 General contextual background to the research question

Although it has been a well established tradition that academic researchers should find their new research questions in the extant literature, in recent years it has become acceptable that a research question could originate from a practical situation. Whatever the source of the research question it is likely that it will be strongly focused. There are many advantages to having a focused question. In

---

[16] A random sample would not be relevant here as the researcher is looking only for individuals who have knowledge of the research area and thus may have an opinion which is worth incorporating in the data.

[17] This statement will not be universally agreed by the academic research community. Those who regard a focus group as a multiple interviewing opportunity will object.

fact it is sometimes argued that without a strong focus academic research will not achieve the desired result which is a contribution to the body of theoretical knowledge. However research questions need to be contextualised and it is not always easy for the academic researcher to do this. One of the techniques for acquiring the requisite knowledge to contextualise a research question is to establish a focus group and to record the conversation of the group on issues related to it.

In this case it is anticipated that the main deliverable from the focus group will be a better understanding of the contextual background to the research question. This is used to support the assertion that the research question is appropriate and answerable. Otherwise the focus group output might actually suggest an alternative research question.

A case in point is the use of evaluation techniques in investment analysis. There are many different approaches to being able to assess the performance of an investment including the numerous qualitative techniques using paybacks and or time value of money techniques. But there are also techniques which use opinion based surveys as well as the view of management strategists. Which technique is appropriate will depend on the context of the organisation and a focus group can be helpful in matching the techniques to the research question.

2.5 Generating testable propositions or hypotheses

Having clarified the main research question the next step is usually to create a series of sub-questions which will in turn lead to propositions or hypotheses. Allowing a focus group to discuss what might be appropriate propositions or hypotheses can be useful.

The focus group is especially useful here because there are often many different possible sub-questions for any given research question. In turn in answering each sub-question there maybe a number of questionnaire or interview schedule level questions which could be asked. Researchers have often found that these issues discussed by a focus group will be helpful in deciding on the content and structure of the final measuring instrument.

2.6 Eliciting issues and factors around a specific topic

Researchers can be quite sure about the field of study they wish to explore but they can be quite vague as to exactly which topic offers the best avenue for successful research. A focus group may sometimes turn up ideas related to issues which are part of the back drop of the main research topic. It is the exchange between the focus group members which sometimes lead to this type of discovery.

Considering the field of investment evaluation again there are issues related to the frequency with which organisations undertake such evaluation exercises. There is also the question relating to the fact that some organisations do not perform any investment evaluation at all. These are only some of the issues which surround the issue of investment evaluation which will profit from a focus group discussion.

2.7 Field testing or piloting a measuring instrument

Any measuring instrument or interview schedule needs to be field tested as the researcher can often become too close to his or her work to be able to see what ambiguities have crept into the research instrument. Field testing may be performed individually or with a group of people such as a focus group. The focus group has the advantage that the members can talk to each other about how they are experiencing the measuring instrument and this can lead to a much richer feed back to the researcher[18].

2.8 Interpreting the findings of the research

Interpreting the findings is sometimes said to be one of the most challenging aspects of an academic research project. It is certainly

---

[18] Some researchers argue that this application of a focus group is quite close to the concept of a multiple interview and if it only involved bringing a number of people together to complete a questionnaire this would certainly be the case. The opportunity afforded the individuals to discuss the questions and make recommendations is what makes this meeting into a focus group.

one of the most creative aspects of this work. It may not always be obvious to the researcher what the implications of his or her research findings are. This may be because the researcher has become too close to the detailed work which has been required up to this stage of the research. Once again a focus group, bringing together a number of different minds and different views can be important to flesh out a more comprehensive understanding of the research results and how they may affect practice in the field being studied. Focus group members can supply important insights which are not obvious to the researcher.

2.9 Multiple voices

An important aspect of a focus group is the fact that it provides the researcher with the opportunity to hear multiple voices and the interaction between them, on a particular subject. Multiple voices frequently provide a richer understanding than even the most knowledgeable single voice. From a philosophical point of view this is what drives the dialectic and make it such an important learning activity. The focus group can thus be seen as a dialectic type activity.

In addition this multiple voice aspect of a focus group meeting can have the effect of allowing participants to develop their own ideas and then share them. It has often been said that individuals do not really know what they think until they have said it. Clarifications and reflections on what individuals say can easily occur in the non-threatening environment of a focus group. Furthermore because a number of people are discussing the subject a focus group is sometimes seen as a way of obtaining multiple opinions quickly and easily.

2.10 The sample and sampling frame

The individuals attending a focus group can be considered to be a sample and this would be a purposeful sample. The researcher needs to create a sampling frame listing the people which he or she would like to have present. It may be that the researcher would like to have a number of different focus groups for example one consisting of Senior Management, one consisting of Middle Management and one consisting of Junior Management. In this case three sampling frames would be required.

Identifying the individuals who should comprise a focus group is not a trivial task. They need to be knowledgeable about the issues to be discussed as well as being prepared to discuss these issues openly within a group which may not necessarily agree with their opinions. Many academic focus groups require individuals who are relatively senior in their organisations and it can be quite difficult for them to find the time to attend such a group.

2.11 Size and time

Some research sources suggest that it is possible or even preferable to conduct focus groups of 8 to 12 individuals[19]. This may be correct when focus groups are being conducted for market research purposes. But for academic research a smaller group is preferable. Most researchers will want to work with between 6 and 8 participants in the group. More than 8 will make the event difficult to manage[20].

The duration of a focus group should be between 60 and 90 minutes. After 90 minutes the participants and the facilitator or researcher are likely to be tired and will thus be less effective. Focus group events of less than 60 minutes are unlikely to have been able to discuss the subject in the depth required. A focus group of less than 60 minutes may be seen by potential informants as not being adequate for a comprehensive discussion and thus not worthy of participating.

---

[19] With some experience and with the support of an assistant larger focus groups could be entertained. It is important not to over stretch in this respect as large focus groups are difficult to manage and if the group discussion gets out of control the value of the event will be diminished.

[20] Focus groups of 4 to 6 people are sometimes referred to as a mini focus group. It is not possible to know how many people will actually turn up on the day and thus it is wise to invite a few more than you need to run the focus group.

Some researchers would like the focus group to address a number of issues or questions. The type of questions which are usually asked and the ability of the participants to discuss these in some detail can mean that only 3 to 4 questions[21] can be handled at one sitting of the group. It is not common to be able to recall a focus group for a second meeting.

2.12 Pre-existing groups

Researchers sometimes wish to obtain opinions from pre-existing groups such as an ICT Steering Committee, Strategic Planning Committee or a Blue Sky Planning group. This type of group could also be members of a Chamber of Commerce or Special Interest Groups of a Computer Society or members of a Watchdog Consumer Panel for example. Such groups could supply important information to the researcher but there are problems in working with these types of groups. The first issue is whether members of this type of group will be prepared to discuss the questions openly. Pre-existing groups will often have members at different levels in the corporate hierarchy and which could inhibit open discussion. The second issue relates to obtaining an undertaking of confidentiality from the members of the group not to disclose who said what. With pre-existing groups this may be difficult to obtain and it may not be easy for the members to comply with this undertaking[22]. In addition with pre-existing groups which are sometimes referred to as private groups there is the issue that the range of opinions which exist may be reduced as all the members are likely to have, at least, to some extent common experiences.

2.13 Evidence available from a focus group

The researcher should create a transcript of the focus group discussion[23]. This will be developed from notes taken by the researcher as

---

[21] There may be some or even many sub-questions within the main questions.

[22] If something is said which is directly pertinent to their work they may need to pass this information on.

[23] It is at least in theory possible for a researcher to work directly from memory and not need to create a transcript. However this is a most unlikely way to approach

well as transcribing a voice recording or video recording of the meeting. As the objective of the focus group is to acquire insights from the opinions and attitudes of the individuals present this transcript seldom contains much factual information, although sometimes a participant may reveal some factual details about the situation. Where facts surface then the researcher should subsequently validate them by further research.

The aim of the focus group is to acquire opinions, beliefs, experiences and descriptions. In business and management studies these opinions can be more helpful than simple facts as they can give the researcher insights into issues which motivated the organisation and the individuals to undertake the activities being studied. Provided they are recognised for what they are it is not always necessary to try to externally validate opinions.

Sometimes the verbal exchanges between participants can become argumentative and the researcher needs to be aware of this and intervene if necessary.

The researcher should be attentive to points of agreement and points of disagreement and note these specifically.

As well as focusing on the conversation the researcher should be making field notes in which he or she may record details of body language and facial expression and perhaps tone of voice. After a 90 minute focus group a researcher may have a dozen or more pages of notes and a recording which will produce a 25 to a 30 page transcription. Of course the length of the transcription will depend on the speed of talking and opinion interchanging among the members of the group. Inevitably a focus group will result in a substantially sized transcript requiring a considerable amount of analytical work.

The nature of the data or evidence obtained through the use of a focus group is unlike any other evidence which is acquired during an

---

academic research and it would directly impact the validity and reliability of the research.

academic research process[24]. As mentioned above the emphasis is not on collecting facts as the focus group is designed to go deeper than facts by provoking discussion or debate or even controversy. Researchers look towards this type of data as a means of obtaining a greater or deeper understanding of the issues as well as the motivations of the people involved. Opinions supplied at a focus group may be seen as clues to the underlining motivation about which informants may be reluctant to talk openly. Also under the auspices of a discussion the activities and results of the interventions being studied may become clearer as focus group members engage in dialogue.

As with other types of data collection the researcher needs to give thought as to how the data will be analysed in advance of the data

collection activity[25]. Thus as part of the focus group protocol it is important for the researcher to have considered how the focus group transcript will be prepared for analysis. There should be a clear view as to how the data acquired in this way will be used in answering the research question. Focus groups should not be a *nice-to-do* part of the research.

2.14 The facilitator or moderator

A focus group needs a facilitator who is sometimes referred to as a moderator, which in academic research is normally the researcher himself or herself. In the academic research environment the facilitator is not expected to engage in the discussion. The facilitator ini-

---

[24] Some researchers will point out that during an ethnographic study the researcher may observe debates or discussions between the members of the community which are being studied. This ad hoc debate and discussion will be informal and will usually be brief. The researcher may not necessarily have recording equipment on hand and the participants in this type of situation may not wish to be recorded.

[25] Some researchers will argue that the more planning done at this stage the tighter a straight jacket the researcher will eventually wear. There is always a choice to be made between being unprepared and thus obtaining little useful data and being too prepared and thus not being aware of the nuances to which a more open approach will be receptive.

tiates the discussion and then steps back while the focus group participants engage in the conversation. The facilitator needs to summarise the discussion but not to make a direct contribution.

The facilitator normally only intervenes if the group strays off the topic and begins to discuss issues not of direct relevance to the research topic. It is difficult for the facilitator to know how much latitude to give the discussion. Clearly if the focus group members begin to discuss a subject of no relevance to the research then some action is required. A simple reminder of the research question being addressed may be enough in such cases.

Sometimes certain members of the group become dominant in the discussion and the facilitator may intervene to encourage others to speak and thus balance this situation. On other occasions members of the focus group may not be adequately forthcoming with their opinions and the facilitator may want to draw them out and would directly ask them for a view on the topic. Most focus groups generate an interesting and positive interaction between the members participating. Occasionally there may be some friction between individuals who take contrary views. Sometimes one member may even try to bully another. When any type of inappropriate behaviour occurs the facilitator needs to intervene.

Rarely, a member of a focus may make politically incorrect comments which can lead to offence and thus antagonise other members. If this happens it is up to the facilitator to intervene and rectify the situation. In extreme cases where considerable offence has been given an apology may not be sufficient and the facilitator may have to ask a member to leave or even dissolve the group. Fortunately this is a rare occurrence.

With regards the summarisation of a focus group's deliberations it may be desirable to pause the discussion every 10 or 15 minutes and summarise what has been said and establish if any conclusions have been reached. Written notes need to be taken at each of these pauses. In addition to this a final summary is required at the end of the event. In order to do this successfully the facilitator will need to be listening carefully to the discussion and also be taking appropriate notes.

2.15 Planning the focus group

The planning of a focus group is not a trivial matter and this activity may take hours or even days (Krueger and Casey 2009). The creation of a focus group protocol is a helpful first step in this planning process. There is an example of such a protocol in Exhibit 2.1 at the end of the Chapter.

There are a number of steps which have to be carefully planned before being able to run a focus group in order that the process of the event is coherent. These are:-

2.15.1 What questions will be put to the focus group?

An important factor in having an effective focus group is preparing appropriate questions. A list of about 4 questions is normally created. An example list is shown in Exhibit 2.2. It is customary to start with a relatively simple and general question and then advance to more specific and complex ones. Each question has to address some aspect of the research question or the context of the research question or the implications of the research findings. Time spent discussing issues which do not address the research question directly is wasted. It is important not to use focus group time on *wouldn't it be nice to know* questions.

2.15.2 Where will the focus group meet?

If the event can be arranged on the campus in a suitable room it will produce the correct level of required formality. The size of the room available can dictate the number of informants or participants invited. If possible a round table should be used. It would be helpful if the university can supply some refreshments.

2.15.3 What sort of participants will be required?

Academic researchers would often like to have access to leaders in the field of study and frequently this is not possible. It is important to be realistic as to who would accept an invitation to your focus group. Sometimes an invitee will suggest a substitute for himself or herself and such a person can occasionally turn out to be ideal for the focus group. Serendipity works even at this level of detail.

2.15.4 Who will be invited to participate?

With the above point in mind, create a list of the people who you feel might accept an invitation to attend a focus group. The invitation could be verbal or in writing. Verbal invitations should be followed by a written one. Use the university letterhead for this purpose. It is probable that an academic researcher may require a gatekeeper to introduce him or her to the appropriate organisations and people. If this is so then write to both the prospective focus group member and to the gatekeeper who helped you indentify the possible informant.

The invitation should explain who you are and the objective of your research. The main research question should be stated together with the question with which you intend to launch the focus group discussion.

The invitation should also state where the focus group will be held, at what time it will commence and how long it is likely to take. Exhibit 2.3 contains such a letter of invitation.

2.15.5 The rules of the focus group meeting

It is important to create a list of the rules for the focus group meeting and supply these to the members before the meeting begins. The rules will state that only one person may speak at a time; that the facilitator needs to give permission for anyone to speak; that the time to speak will be carefully managed; that the Chatham House rule applies etc. (see footnote 20 to paragraph 2.19)

2.15.6 Other invitation issues

Make sure sufficient lead time is given to reduce the possibility that potential focus group members will be previously engaged. It is also useful to give a few alternate dates and to say if none of these are suitable the potential participant can nominate his or her own preferred date for the meeting.

Do not invite people who might be uncomfortable in each other's company such as individuals from competitive organisations[26]. Except where a pre-existing group may be involved it is also important not to invite junior and senior people from the same organisation as this can have the effect of inhibiting open conversation. As mentioned before a junior member may be embarrassed to express an opinion in front of a senior executive from the same organisation.

Follow up these invitations to obtain a firm commitment to attend the focus group. Remembering that number required for the event is 6 to 8 people and that there are frequently drop outs or no shows at the last minute, due to urgent business arising during the day, it is always better to ensure that there are 8 acceptances.

2.16 Inter-organisational and intra-organisational focus groups

An intra-organisational focus group is one where the members of the group are all from the same organisation. The pre-existing groups mentioned above are sometimes intra-organisational but not always. This type of group may be useful if the researcher is conducting a case study and is seeking to establish information about how a certain event was perceived by the staff. This type of discussion could have a similar effect to engaging in an informant triangulation exercise. With such a group it is important to bear in mind that individuals of approximately the same seniority in the organisation should be invited as it can be problematic for senior staff to openly discuss corporate events at a meeting attended by junior or even middle management. The same, of course, applies to junior or middle management speaking freely in front of senior management. Therefore care needs to be taken to avoid potentially uncomfortable situations arising for members of the focus group.

---

[26] The individuals may be sufficiently savvy to ask the question: Who else has been invited? And they may ask for an assurance that no one from a competitive firm will be present.

An inter-organisational focus group is one where the members of the group are from different organisations. A group composed of individuals like this would be useful in obtaining information concerning industry trends or movements. Here the facilitator needs to be aware that individuals from competitive organisations will often refuse to discuss organisationally sensitive matters in front of each other. In the letter of invitation to potential focus group participants it is important to indicate the types of individuals you are inviting to that focus group meeting. Therefore care needs to be taken to avoid any potential conflict of interests arising as participants from competitive firms may just walk out of the meeting.

Remember that the quality of the data obtained from a focus group is dependent on the atmosphere of the meeting being relaxed and non-threatening. The inclusion of inappropriate individuals can ruin the whole event.

2.17 The focus group meeting

A focus group may be seen to have four steps. The first is the welcoming and the opening and introductions; the second is the facilitator explaining the procedures; the third is the discussions; the fourth is the debriefing and the thanks and farewells.

2.17.1 Welcoming and the opening and introductions

The researcher should individually welcome each participant and remind them of what the research is seeking to achieve and why this is important. Everyone needs to be introduced to each other. Name badges should be supplied. The researcher may read a Welcoming Statement such as is shown in Exhibit 2.4.

2.17.2 Explaining the procedures

The facilitator should restate the questions to be discussed. Rules such as only one person should speak at a time need to be explained. Sometimes participants are asked to state their name before they speak so that the transcription from the voice recording will be easier. The Research Participants' Information Document shown in Exhibit 2.5 and the Letter of Consent shown in Exhibit 2.6

should be presented. The facilitator should collect a signed copy of the Letter of Consent from each focus group member.

2.17.3 The discussions

The facilitator should start the discussion by posing the first question. If the conversation does not start naturally from that point the facilitator may engage in a limited amount of prompting but this should be carefully curtailed as it may have an undue influence on the discussion. The facilitator needs to keep time carefully so all the questions will have a fair share of the time available. It is important that the facilitator keeps notes of the main points discussed and any areas of controversy encountered. These need to be read to the participants during the debriefing session.

2.17.4 Paper exercises

Sometimes it may be appropriate for the facilitator to ask the focus group members to undertake a paper exercise. An example of this is where the facilitator would like the group to indicate their preferences for a certain policy or process or individual. A list of these could be provided on paper and the members could be asked to indicate their order of preference by numbering them from one to the largest number of items presented.

2.17.5 Debriefing and the thanks and farewells

Debriefing is an important aspect of the focus group and time should be made available to conduct this properly. The facilitator should restate the research question and then read the individual questions discussed summarising the main points made and any differences in opinion raised during the discussion. Focus group members should then be invited to point out any omissions or misunderstanding which the facilitator may have made. Careful note needs to be taken of these. The facilitator then needs to reiterate the fact that focus group members may withdraw their comments if they wish and supply the members with his or her contact details.

2.17.6 In an ideal world

In an ideal world a focus group should really run itself but this seldom happens. The lighter the touch on the rudder by the facilitator the better the result will be. The researcher needs to collect all the notes taken and the audio or video recording of the meeting and produce a transcript as soon as possible. As the researcher's memory is a key element of the data which has been acquired there should not be any sizeable delay in producing the transcript.

2.18 A field note to reflect on the focus group

As soon as possible after the focus group meeting the researcher should write a field note reflection on what was said by whom and who had the strongest arguments. This field note will be particularly useful when the transcript of the focus group is written up. The importance of reflection was expressed by Weick (1979) when he said:

> *All understanding originates in reflection and looking backwards.*

The notion of reflection has become increasingly important in business and management research. The reflection can be facilitated by the researcher using the structure for a field note by answering the questions in Exhibit 2.7.

2.19 Ethics committee

Academic research increasingly requires the approval of an Ethics Committee if any contact with people is involved. A focus group would be considered as constituting an event for which ethics approval is required. Ethics committees usually meet periodically (sometimes only once per quarter) and thus application to the committee should be made well in advance of the date planned for the focus group. Many universities will not countenance retrospective applications for ethics approval.

In the case of a focus group, before the discussion can take place Ethics Committee requirements have to be attended to. As mentioned above each member of the focus group has to be presented with a Research Participants' Information Document. Allow 5 to 10 minutes for this document to be read and answer any questions which are raised. Then offer the informant a copy of a Letter of Consent to sign. Make it especially clear that anything said will be held in total confidence by the researcher.

In addition to the researcher giving a confidentiality undertaking to the informants, in the case of focus groups the researcher needs to ask all the members of the group to agree to respect the confidentiality of the opinions of each other. Focus groups normally operate in terms of the Chatham House Rule[27]. This rule states that the opinions expressed during the meeting should not be attributed to any particular person. If members of the group hear any interesting ideas which may be of use to them or their organisation they are of course at liberty to use such information but the source of specific comments and opinions are protected. The Chatham House Rule needs to be stated in the Letter of Consent.

Ethics committees are particularly concerned if the researcher wishes to work with individuals who are perceived to come from vulnerable groups. Vulnerable groups are not easy to define but they include children, the elderly and disabled individuals. However some researchers and ethics committees believe that in relation to their employers all employees should be considered as vulnerable. This is rather an extreme position which would not be accepted by all researchers.

---

[27] The rule states that members of a meeting may not attribute what they have said to one another. Members of the meeting may use the information they acquire at the meeting without attribution. According to the Chatham House website, "The Chatham House Rule originated at Chatham House [in the UK] with the aim of providing anonymity to speakers and to encourage openness and the sharing of information. It is now used throughout the world as an aid to free discussion. Meetings do not have to take place at Chatham House, or be organised by Chatham House, to be held under the Rule. Meetings, events and discussions held at Chatham House are normally conducted 'on the record' with the Rule occasionally invoked at the speaker's request. In cases where the Rule is not considered sufficiently strict, an event may be held 'off the record'".
http://www.chathamhouse.org.uk/about/chathamhouserule/

Some relatively introverted members of a focus group could be vulnerable to more outgoing members and it is possible for the outgoing members to be belittling of the view of those who are not as articulate as themselves. The ethics protocol should show that the researcher is aware of this potential problem and has thought about what can be done if this situation arrives.

2.20 There are no right or wrong answers

It is important that the facilitator emphasise that in the discussion there are no right or wrong answers, but rather opinions and that everyone's opinion will be held in the same high regard. There are however boundaries as to what is required to be discussed and if the conversation goes beyond these boundaries then useful data will not be obtained. Informants need to be aware of the boundaries and it is the facilitator's task to remind them of these if they wander away from the subject area.

2.21 Limited intervention of the facilitator

Not all focus groups run seamlessly with continuous conversation and sometimes the facilitator may have to continually restate questions or expand on their implications. But this is relatively uncommon especially if the members of the group have been chosen with care.

Focus groups should not be allowed to overrun by any substantial amount of time but it is not essential to stop abruptly when the time expires. If the group is deeply involved in discussion the facilitator can ask if members are prepared to stay a little longer. It should be recognised that focus group participation can be quite stressful and tiring.

Some facilitators end a focus group by asking the members to write down any important conclusions which have been reached during the discussion but this is optional.

When it is time to end the meeting the facilitator should thank the group and if they are interested he or she may offer them an electronic copy of the research findings. When focus groups are run by market researchers they are often offered a small gift or a small amount of money at the end of the meeting but this is seldom appropriate with academic research. A letter of thanks should be sent to each member of the group within the following few days. An example is provided in Exhibit 2.8.

If the facilitator has been observing body language or physical gestures etc he or she should write up their field notes as soon as the participants have left so as not to forget these details.

2.22 Virtual focus groups - telephone and online

Some researchers have argued that a focus group could be conducted either over the telephone, using a conference call, or online over the internet. These have been referred to as virtual focus groups. Virtual focus groups can save time and cost less to run than the usual form of physical focus group. In academic research because of the nature of the questions and the depth of thought usually required, it would be difficult to justify the use of these approaches as they would not capture much if anything of the rich data which is acquired by person-to-person contact which is achieved during normal focus groups[28]. Also Delphi studies[29] are sometimes regarded as a type of focus group but this type of study seeks consensus from its members and this is not the objective of a focus group. Also the Delphi approach requires a number of rounds which is not part of the focus group method.

---

[28] This view of the superiority of the physical focus group is receding due to the uptake of what is being called e-Research. e-Research refers to the use of a wide spectrum of Internet and Web based tools to support academic research endeavours. One of these tools is video conferencing which may be used in facilitating a focus group.

[29] A Delphi study uses a panel of experts who communicate by the completion of a questionnaire which is centrally processed by a facilitator. The Delphi study usually tries to anticipate developments in technology or management and the name Delphi is used to indicate this. Delphi studies will often use 20 to 30 participants and run for three rounds of the same questions in order to seek consensus. A Delphi study will have a large dropout rate of the three rounds of maybe as much as 30 to 40% of the original informants.

In general, telecommunications technology has extended the reach of academic researchers but care needs to be taken when it is incorporated directly into the research process as it is often impersonal and thus does not provide rich results.

2.23 Impromptu focus groups

In an academic environment a group of researchers can spontaneously begin a discussion on a subject of special interest to one of the researchers. Sometimes this can amount to there being an impromptu focus group. A researcher may use the data he or she collects from such a group. For this to succeed the researcher will need to be able to record as many of the points made as possible and then write up a transcript as soon as possible after the impromptu meeting.

2.24 Multiple focus groups

Sometimes a research project requires multiple focus groups. It may be that the researcher would like the opinion of all the senior managers in a particular division of an organisation. If this number was larger than could be handled at one session then multiple focus groups would be required. At the conclusion of each event a transcript would be created and these different transcripts would be analysed and interpreted separately. It would not be good practice to create a super-transcript from the notes and recordings of a number of focus groups as each focus group has its own dynamic and this substantially determines the data produced in the groups.

2.25 Focus groups in different languages

Sometimes a researcher may feel that a focus group conducted in a different language may be useful. There is no fundamental rule prohibiting this. However to be able to use this data in academic research it is important that considerable care be given to the selection of the interpreter and facilitator. Numerous problems can arise in the interpretation and the translation of the data and the researcher would be expected to know about these and have strategies with which to prevent or manage them.

Simply being bilingual will often not be adequate to capture the meaning of the questions put and the answers offered. Thus it is quite probable that the researcher will not be able to acquire as thorough an understanding of the transcript as he or she would have obtained if the interview had been conducted in the researcher's mother tongue. The problem which arises is a cultural one. Sometimes the concepts in which the researcher is interested do not exist is the same way in the other culture and thus no direct translation is possible. In such cases a language-cultural translation is required and when dealing with a focus group it is difficult to ensure the authenticity of this type of exchange of ideas.

Working across languages and cultures is always difficult and the cost of interpreters can often be high and the processes involved with the translation will slow down the research. For most academic purposes working across languages and cultures is a complication and which should only be undertaken with considerable care.

2.26 The output/outcome from a focus group

The physical output of a focus group will be the notes taken by the facilitator and the copy of the audio or video recording taken. The next step is to create a transcript of the event using the hand written notes and the recordings. The transcript should be enriched by any field note taken. The second step is to choose a method of analysis. There are several approaches available the most important of which are content analysis and hermeneutic analysis. There are a number of tools available to assist with this which include coding, perceptual mapping, cross tabulation etc. Correspondence[30] analysis is sometimes helpful in this respect.

[30] Correspondence analysis was developed in France and thus the word is French meaning connection. It is currently available in a number of statistical packages and it produces new insights using qualitative data. The original spelling for the name of the technique was the French correspondence.

2.27 Challenges offered by focus groups

There are several challenges which the researcher faces in conducting competent focus groups. It can be difficult to find appropriate individuals to join the focus group. The type of people required will often consider they are too busy to attend such an event. This may or may not be an excuse. Some people will simply not want to share their view as part of a group as they think that this might be too open and there could be some competitive advantage lost by doing this.

Scheduling everyone's diaries so that the entire group will be available at the same time can be problematic. By offering a substantial lead time in the invitation the researcher can help ameliorate this. But sometimes the researcher would like to have a quick short focus group to help with some problem in the research and this is not always possible.

Without recording the proceedings it can be difficult to construct a transcript and sometimes members of the focus group will not give permission for themselves to be recorded. A single dissenting voice will require a decision of either exclusion or no recording.

Finding a suitable assistant to help with the focus group can sometimes be difficult. Researchers typically do not have administrative help and usually have to rely on friendships for such assistance.

With regards to the actual conversation which takes place during the focus group there can sometimes be a pseudo-consensus with informants being too polite to disagree in front of each other. Some people find it too stressful to argue in a group and thus they sit back and appear to agree when in fact they don’t. Some participants will even lie. The researcher is expected to watch out for this by observing body language and tone of voice and this is not always possible.

2.28 Issues of which to be aware

The facilitator can find that he or she is spending too much time intervening to sort out definitions or to prevent misunderstandings occurring between members of the group. Thus the time allowed for the focus group can go by quickly without achieving all that the researcher wished. It can be difficult to have the same focus group reconvene at a later time to continue the discussion.

As stated before participants may be reluctant to provide their true opinions in front of other focus group members. Evaluating the responses for their sincerity can be difficult. There is the temptation that the researcher will cherry pick the views of the participants to suit his or her own agenda. Even when the researcher is being careful and trying to minimise his or her bias this can easily happen.

It is difficult to create an authentic transcript of a focus group without recording what has been said. In fact if it is possible it is better to video the focus group session as that will help the researcher recall the tone of voice, the body language and other non-verbal cues. However to do this it will be necessary to obtain permission from the group as a whole and this may not be forthcoming. If one person objects to the video recording then it cannot be used unless the researcher decides to proceed without that person. Also if it is intended to use video recording then this needs to be stated in the ethics protocol.

2.29 Has the focus group been successful?

When the event has been completed and the transcript written up the researcher should reflect on whether the focus group has been successful, i.e. have objectives set by the researcher for the focus group been achieved. This is done by asking the questions:-

- Did new issues surface during the discussions of the focus group?
- What was confirmed by the focus group?
- Were there any misunderstandings or even myths dispelled by the focus group?
- What has been learnt about conducting a focus group which will make it easier for the researcher to conduct the next one?

A successful focus group will produce a substantial list of answers and or suggestions which are pertinent to these questions.

The answers to these questions can help move the research forward considerably. Sometimes a focus group can be responsible for redefining the research question or adding to or reducing the list of subquestions. On other occasions the focus group will make the context of the research much clearer. However it is not the intention that the focus group output will answer the research question itself. It is important to remember that, as the focus group has been created to seek opinions and insights as a result of a discussion or debate between its members, the data obtained from it may have a low level of factual content.

Some researchers ask if focus group data can be considered to be valid and reliable. These particular terms are more correctly applicable to quantitative research. In qualitative research these aspects of research are better articulated as creditable and dependable. Thus one can ask has the focus group been conducted in such a way that the results may be regarded as creditable and dependable. For the results to be creditable it is necessary to have had appropriate informants or discussants at the focus group. There needs to have been an adequate number of people present and a clear and well articulated set of questions need to have been used. In addition the facilitator needs to have been competent. Ideally the facilitator should have been the researcher himself or herself.

For the focus group results to be regarded as dependable then the recording of the proceedings, i.e. the discussions of the group, need to have been competently recorded and transcribed with care. The questions need not only be appropriate but they also need to be completely unambiguous. In addition the dependability of the results would be improved if the facilitator has at least one assistant with him or her during the focus group meeting to help with the work involved.

2.30 Reflections on focus groups for academic research

Before concluding a chapter on focus groups it is appropriate to reflect on the assumptions and the values which drive the use of focus groups in academic research.

Focus groups for academic research

To conduct an academic focus group a researcher brings together a group of knowledgeable informants and asks them to debate an issue which is central to answering the research question. Although researchers differ somewhat on this point, many would agree that the primary purpose of the academic focus group is not to collect simple data. The objective of the focus group is to listen to a discussion or debate or discourse among the knowledgeable informants and thus to learn about how the issues are viewed or understood by different knowledgeable informants. This is different to what we normally regard as data and some researchers may regard this as less valuable than normal data. The understandings which the researcher takes away from the focus group will normally be richer than simple data.

In academic research the focus group should be seen as a type of barometer which gives the researcher an indication as to whether he or she is on the right track and thus likely to produce interesting findings. If the researcher strays off the required route then it is likely that there will be trouble later on in the research process in arguing that the research has produced something of value.

One of the implications of the above is that if the focus group is conducted correctly and if the researcher is the facilitator or mediator then the transcript itself is probably an adequate outcome of the event. This is in contrast to interview transcripts where a considerable amount of analysis may be required. This does not imply that it is easy to understand the transcript and considerable reflection may be necessary. A focus group well conducted may make a substantial difference to the thinking of the researcher.

As a final reflection on the nature of focus groups the description above is sometimes regarded as being too prescriptive. Some researchers would argue that conducting a focus group in a more open way, i.e. without a list of questions, can also be valuable. In such a case it is argued that the agenda will emerge as the informants discuss the issues which are important to them. No doubt this can sometimes be the case but it is a riskier approach to the one outlined above. As mentioned earlier focus groups are difficult to assemble, manage and to understand their meaning and thus they should not be undertaken lightly.

2.31 Summary and conclusion

Focus groups are an important technique in academic research which many researchers will want to use. They are especially useful in acquiring reflected opinions from informants as these opinions are at least to some extent honed in the debate or discussion which is part of the focus group. Although there is some disagreement on this issue, focus groups should not be seen as simply an approach to multiple interviewing as the discussion between the informants is important to the researcher. It is not the purpose of a focus group to arrive at a consensus.

It is most important to select appropriate questions for the focus group. These questions should be developed with the research question firmly in mind.

When researchers first hear of focus groups this technique can appear to be an easy way of gathering data from a number of individuals quickly. However this is seldom the case. It is not easy to assemble a useful group of individuals who are prepared to share their opinions. The types of individuals required for a useful focus group are likely to be highly committed and busy managers or executives with little spare time. Therefore it is important to plan a focus group well ahead of the date of the proposed event. Sometimes it is appropriate in the letter of invitation to ask the informant to suggest an alternative individual if he or she is unable to be free for the event on the date suggested. The researcher has to be careful that the substitute person proposed in this way has the knowledge to participate in the discussion required.

If the researcher has to pay for a meeting room and for refreshments, this can be costly. The researcher as facilitator has to be able to manage several things at once and thus needs an assistant. This could be a problem as assistants do not usually come free.

Some researchers are not naturally good focus group facilitators and this can mean that the output of the focus group is not as useful as it could be. There are a number of organisations advertised on the web which offer to facilitate a focus group for a researcher. However these have to be reviewed with considerable caution as they may not be fully familiar with the requirements of academic focus groups and may not capture the data which the academic researcher requires. When an aspect of an academic researchers' work is outsourced then the researcher has to carefully manage all aspects of this work. It is possible that non-academics will not understand all aspects of the requirement.

The creation of the transcript can be difficult and even when it has been recorded it can be challenging to recognise voices and thus recall who said what during the focus group meeting. Conversational speech will inevitably have many "ums" and "ahws" which need to be extracted from the text. Sometimes impolite and unacceptable language may have to be modified or at least the offending words omitted. On the other hand if the focus group is well managed this technique can bring together highly experienced individuals who can substantially assist in clarifying issues for the researcher and in so doing add new insights and thereby contribute to answering the research question.

2.32 Traps to avoid

It is important that researchers do not perceive a focus group to be a multiple interview. The type of data which a researcher receives from a person in a one-to-one interview is quite different from the type of data which will be provided as a result of a focus group. Focus groups tap a different level of consciousness to that which an interview can normally access. Sometimes members of a focus group will argue contrary to their beliefs in order to probe the understanding of other members of the group. Sometime they will do this just for the sake of having a good argument. On the other hand members of a focus group may become bored and appear to agree when they do not. In using a focus group it is important that the researcher does not assume that "silence means consent".

As focus groups are not aimed at achieving consensus no attempt should be made to draw an agreed conclusion from the group. The data is often more powerful when more issues and disagreements have surfaced.

It is not possible to make any generalisations from the data acquired from a focus group and any attempt to so do will lead to validity and replication problems.

Focus groups are sometimes seen as an opportunity to collect data by having a friendly chat with people that the researcher knows. This is a complete misunderstanding of what a focus group intends to achieve. Universities generally do not offer any skills training in focus groups and thus the data obtained from focus groups should be carefully examined before being accepted as part of the evidence for an academic degree.

In general focus groups are often used naively in academic research.

2.33 End note

To conclude here are the 12 principles for making focus groups work in academic research.

1. Carefully plan all aspects of the focus group using the Focus Group Protocol provided at the end of this Chapter.
2. Make sure that whoever is invited to the focus group is knowledgeable about the topic and prepared to discuss it with others.
3. Do not mixed senior and middle or junior individuals in the same group as this may cause the not so senior people to be reluctant to offer an opinion.
4. Do not expect that all those who have accepted invitations to attend will show up on the day. Perhaps invite one or two more than you really need. Remember that a focus group of 4 to 6 people is manageable. But even then an assistant is helpful.
5. Ensure all the necessary introductions are made; state the requirement of confidentiality from all parties and the other is-

sues in the ethics protocol and obtain signed letters of consent. Obtain permission to record the focus group meeting.

6. Pose the question or questions to the group.
7. Facilitate the focus group meeting as unobtrusively as possible. Only intervene if the focus group strays off course or if there is a difficulty between some individuals.
8. Become accomplished at active listening.
9. Keep the timing that has been agreed in advance.
10. Thank the informants for participating in the focus group and ask for permission to telephone them with points of clarification later.
11. Create field notes or make entries in a field diary as soon as possible after the focus group.
12. Produce the focus group transcript as soon as possible after the interview.

Exhibits for Chapter Two

Exhibit 2.1: Focus Group Protocol

Item No	Issue	Detail	Notes
1	Research Topic	How IT investment benefits are evaluated	
2	Research question	How to develop the theory of ICT investment analysis so as to incorporate intangible benefits and soft costs	
3	Informant/s	Marketing managers from local SMEs	
4	Location and room layout	University syndicate room A Round table, flip chart and projector	
5	Facilitator	Myself	
6	List of questions	Four questions provided	
7	Arrival at premises	Time to commence 1600 on Thursday 23 July	
8	Assistant	Undergraduate student	
9	Equipment	Digital recorded	
10	Name tags	Each participant has a name tag	
11	Letter	Inviting focus group members	
12	List	List of questions	
13	Papers	Research Participants' Information Document	
14	Papers	Letter of consent	
15	Letter	Thanking members for their contribution	
16	Data/transcript analysis	How will the transcript be analysed? Content analysis Correspondence analysis Hermeneutics	

Exhibit 2.2: Focus Group Discussion Questions

Question No	Issue	Notes
1	What is your opinion of the relevance of this research?	
2	Do you believe that answering the research question will facilitate practitioners being able to have more control over their work function?	
3	In your opinion do you feel that the board of directors will find this issue sufficient to warrant a review of the organisation's policy?	
4	Do you think that this topic is time bound in the sense that it will become less relevant over the next few years?	

If this document is distributed to the focus group members during the meeting, and it is recommended that it is, then it should also include a re-statement of the research topic, research questions and other issues which the researcher wants to bring to the attention of the focus group members.

Exhibit 2.3: Letter/e-mail of invitation to join a focus group

Dear Mr So-and-So

I would like to invite you to join the focus group as part of my research which I am convening on the subject of XXXXXXXX on December XXXX to be held at the XXXX Business School. This focus group will discuss some aspect of this subject. I am inviting you as I understand that you are an authority on this topic and your opinions on this subject would be highly appreciated. No preparation work is required and the focus group will last between 60 and 90 minutes.

I am hoping to hold this focus group meeting at the University at X pm on July X. If this date is not convenient please let me know if you can provide me with another date or send an alternative knowledge informant.

I am a researcher at the Business School registered for a XXXX degree. The title of my research is XXXXXX and my principle research question is XXXXXXXXXXXXX. I expect the result of my research will be valuable to organisations such as your own. My research is part of the general research activity of the School and I am attaching a brochure [or including a URL] which will give you more information about the School.

The focus group will consist of 6 to 8 individuals with similar experience to yourself and any comments made by any members of the group will be treated as confidential. If you participate in the focus group I would be pleased to make the results of the research available to you. I will be asking for your assurance that you will also hold the views of the other members of the group to be confidential.

I will telephone you next week to see if I can supply any further information about this event.

I will be most grateful for your help by participating in this discussion.

Yours sincerely,

Researcher....................................Date

Exhibit 2.4: Focus Group Welcoming Statement

My name is XXXXXXXXXX. I am a researcher in the School of XXXXX at the XXXXX University.

Thank you for agreeing to participate in this focus group which is part of my research design for a degree I am taking or a paper I am writing or both.

My research question is XXXXXXXX

The aspects of my research question which I would like to have you discuss and debate today are listed in the document entitled Focus Group Discussion Questions.

Today I will be acting as the focus group facilitator which means that I will put the questions to you one at a time. I will also attempt to prevent the discussion from wandering off track.

I have a Focus Group Research Participants' Information Document which I would like you all to read now. This will take about 5 minutes.

I would be pleased to answer any questions you may have concerning the content of this document.

If you are in agreement with this document, please sign the Letter of Consent which I am now circulating to you. Please pass the signed copy back to me.

Please remember that only one person should speak at a time.

Also please recognise the Chatham House Rule which is that you may use information you hear at this meeting but you should not attribute it to any specific person.

I hope that you will enjoy the discussion we are about to have

Researcher Date

Exhibit 2.5: Focus Group Participants' Information Document

The purpose of this document is to explain to potential focus group participants the nature of the research which is proposed and the role which he or she is being invited to play in that research.

	Issue	Example Detail
1	Name of Researcher Contact Details If part-time state employers name and address	Tom Jones e-mail address and telephone numbers The XYZ Consulting firm.
2	Title of Research Project	Development of a good practice framework for *creating* a structure test procedure within small to medium sized companies
3	Purpose of the Study	The purpose of this research is to develop a framework identifying the steps which a small to medium sized organisation may undertake to develop a test team structure
4	Description of the Study	The research will take the form of a questionnaire and interviews.
5	Duration of the Study	12 months
6	What is involved and how long will it take?	An open discussion in a group of 6 to 8 individuals on topics related to the research question. A focus group meeting will take approximately 90 minutes
7	Why you have been asked to participate?	You have been asked to partake in this study due to your experience in this field.
8	What will happen to the information which will arise from the discussion?	The information will be held in a confidential manner while the work is being collated. Notes, transcripts and tapes will be kept under lock and key. Following the successful completion of the research all material collected as a result of the focus group will be shredded and/or destroyed.
9	What will be done with the Results of the Study?	The results of the focus group will be reported in the different sections of the research work. This will be done in a completely anonymous manner.

	Issue	Example Detail
10	What are the possible disadvantages ?	There are no costs to you associated with your involvement with this study. It is not envisaged that any negative consequences will accrue to you from your contributions in this research.
11	In what way will the study be beneficial and to whom?	It is hoped that this study will provide a useful framework for small and medium sized companies embarking on a software implementation project where they will have to invest significant resources in the test phase. The framework will detail various options available to the management in establishing a test team.
12	Who has reviewed this Study to ensure that it complies with all the requirements and ethical standards of the university?	The Ethics Committee of the School of Big Black Boxes at the Unitary College Dublin have approved this research proposal and granted permission for the research to commence/continue.
13	Can permission be withdrawn having previously been granted?	Yes, all members of the discussion group shall retain the right to have their contributions to the research withdrawn at any time
14	Can you refuse to answer any question?	Yes. The contributor has the right to refuse to answer any question.
15	Confidentiality within the focus group.	The members of the focus group are requested to respect the confidentiality of all other members of the group and thus not to directly quote the comments made by anyone during the focus group meeting

Exhibit 2.6: Focus Group Letter of Informed Consent

I, Jane Doe, agree voluntarily to take part in the focus group which is part of the research project being conducted by Tom Jones as part of the requirements for his Doctorate/Masters Degree or Research paper at UCD. I have read the Research Participants' Information Document and I understand the contents thereof. Any questions which I have asked have been answered to my satisfaction.

I understand that the information which I will supply is confidential and that it will be anonymised.

I understand that I do not have to answer all the questions which may be put to me. The information which I provide will be held securely until the research has been completed (published) after which it will be destroyed.

The information which I provide will not be used for any other purpose.

I understand that I am entitled to ask for a de-briefing session or a copy of the research at the end of the research project.

I have been informed that I may withdraw from this study at any time and that any information which I have supplied will not be used for this research and any records held relating to my contribution will be destroyed.

I agree to respect the confidentiality of the other members of the focus group and not to quote their words to anyone else. I recognise that the Chatham House Rule applies.

Signed .... Date....................................

Exhibit 2.7: Form to facilitate the field note including reflection required after the focus group meeting

Member name	Participants argument/s	Was it well defended?	Did a new idea emerge?

Exhibit 2. 8: A letter/e-mail of thanks for having participated in a focus group.

Dear Mr So-and-so

I would like to thank you for participating in the focus group which I recently held on the subject of XXXXXXXX on December XXXX at the XXXX Business School.

Your comments have been helpful to my research project.

I would like to re-confirm that your contribution will remain confidential and that all the working papers of my research will be held securely until the project is completed and then they will be destroyed.

If you wish I can e-mail you a copy of my research findings.

Yours sincerely,

Researcher Date

References

Barbour R, 2007, *Doing Focus Groups*, Sage, London

Litselliti L, 2003, *Using Focus Groups in Research*, Continuum, London

Kitzinger J, (1995), "Qualitative Research: Introducing focus groups", BMJ, 311:299

Krueger R, 1988, Focus Groups – A practical guide for applied research, Sage, Newbury Park CA.

Krueger R and A Casey , (2009), Focus groups, Sage, Thousand Oaks, Ca, USA

Richie J and J Lewis, 2003, *Qualitative Research Practice*, Sage London

Weick K, (1979) *The Social Psychology of Organizing*, Addison-Wesley, Reading MA

Useful websites

http://www.bolton.ac.uk/Students/StudyResources/Library/HelpGuides/CribSheets/Focusgroups.pdf

http://www.wikihow.com/Run-a-Focus-Group

http://communication.howstuffworks.com/how-focus-groups-work1.htm

http://www.webcredible.co.uk/user-friendly-resources/web-usability/focus-groups.shtml

http://managementhelp.org/evaluatn/focusgrp.htm

http://www.hse.gov.uk/stress/standards/pdfs/focusgroups.pdf

http://focusgroups.pbworks.com/Issues-including-advantages-and-disadvantages

http://www.evalued.bcu.ac.uk/tutorial/4b.htm

http://en.wikipedia.org/wiki/Focus_group

http://www.programevaluation.org/focusgroups.htm

http://www.focusgroups.uk.com/?gclid=CLrEn_GyxqUCFYUe4QodYl2UOQ

http://www.webcredible.co.uk/user-friendly-resources/web-usability/focus-groups.shtml

http://www.researchvillage.co.uk/focus-group-experts?gclid=CNrY2uWVtacCFUEb4QodClMZAw

http://www.fieldwork-assistance.co.uk/Focus_group.html

Chapter Three Questionnaires for Academic Research

Questionnaires are frequently used in academic research at all levels from undergraduate level projects to postgraduate dissertations for both masters and doctoral degrees. However questionnaires are often poorly designed and not well employed in the research process. Questionnaires are perceived as such a common feature of 21st century society that they are seldom rigorously defined and often little attention is given to the detail required to make these instruments an effective way for the collection of useful research data. Some questionnaires are so badly designed that the data supplied can be of little use for academic purposes. When used correctly questionnaires are a powerful technique in academic research and they deserve close study and careful attention before they are employed.

There is a large number of ways that questionnaires may be designed and used in academic research and this chapter can only look at a limited number of these. Therefore the focus has been placed on general issues which have been supported by some examples.

3.1 Definition

To understand the use of questionnaires it is important to begin with a clear definition. In academic research a questionnaire is a data or evidence collecting device that consists of a list or series of specific questions which when answered by an appropriate informant or group of informants, will help lead a researcher to a greater understanding of the research question/s and provide insight into possible answers. A questionnaire is normally presented as a list of questions in the shape of a form[31] and the data so collected is often,

[31] In academic research the questionnaire is increasingly offered to informants as a computer screen based form which has advantages over the traditional paper based equivalent.

though not always, intended for statistical analysis. A questionnaire may be used to collect a wide range of data concerning the state of affairs of an individual or an organisation or concerning attitude or opinions or beliefs. The research literature sometimes refers to a questionnaire as a measuring instrument and the process of using a questionnaire is referred to as conducting a survey[32]. In order to be a measuring instrument the questionnaire design needs to have identified variables and established how their magnitude might be captured and understood and therefore measured. This is normally achieved through the use of a scale of measurement. Questionnaires are thought to have been first employed in academic research in the 19th century by Francis Galton, a quantitative researcher and so they are often perceived as a way of collecting quantitative data.

Although questionnaires are inclined to require statistical analysis and statistical interpretation, as mentioned above, this need not necessarily be the case. Some questionnaires are designed to be analysed or interpreted in a qualitative way. Also, even when the majority of a questionnaire is quantitative it may also include open or qualitative questions asking the informant for explanations which require a non-statistical approach to analysis. Thus questionnaires can and often do straddle the quantitative-qualitative divide in academic research.

Questionnaires have been considered to be a quick, inexpensive and easy way to collect data. Unfortunately the questionnaire development process requires detailed attention to the requirements of the research and this is not a quick or easy process. Quickly compiled questionnaires are of little use to the academic researcher who may have to discard the data collected by flawed instruments. Furthermore it is increasingly difficult to find informants who will complete

---

[32] The term large scale survey is sometimes used to distinguish a questionnaire from a series of interviews which may be described as an in-depth survey. http://www.socialresearchmethods.net/kb/survtype.php .

a questionnaire for academic research purposes. Using a questionnaire is by no means a quick and easy option.

It has been suggested that the use of a questionnaire is nearly always a compromise. The richest form of data is always obtained by direct contact with the respondent. Direct contact has several advantages including the researchers' ability to observe the appearance of the informant. Here the informant is met in his or her office or home there is further opportunity to observe the informant environment. Tone of voice and body language may also be important and this is cannot be captured through the use of a questionnaire.

3.2 Philosophical underpinning

A questionnaire is only useful in academic research if the researcher believes that the answering of his or her research question may be facilitated by asking the type of questions which can be put to an informant through the medium of a questionnaire. Questionnaires generally contain short structured questions which are answered by ticking a box to indicate the informants' understanding or preference. Sometimes open questions which require written answers are used in questionnaires, but overall the amount of data acquired by the use of a questionnaire is less than that which may be obtained by using other data collection approaches.

The researcher's attitude to questionnaires is rooted in his or her philosophical approach to research. As Hughes (1990) pointed out:-

> *Every research tool or procedure is inextricably embedded in commitments to particular versions of the world and to knowing that world. To use an attitude scale, to take the role of a participant observer, to select a random sample ... is to be involved in conceptions of the world which allow these instruments to be used for the purposes conceived. No technique or method of investigation is self-validating ... they operate only within a given set of assumptions about the nature of society, the nature of human beings, the relationship between the two and how they may be known.*

The consequences of this is that while some researchers favour questionnaires and see them as their data collection approach of choice other believe that questionnaire are not appropriate for academic research in business sand management studies. Those who reject questionnaires usually favour methods such as interviewing, participant-observer journals or action research projects.

3.3 Strategic considerations

Before embarking on the work required in developing or acquiring a competent questionnaire it is important to consider higher level issues relating to whether a questionnaire can be successfully used in the research programme. These issues may be reduced to four questions which are:-

- Is the data that may be obtained through the use of a questionnaire appropriate when answering the research question?
- Who will have to answer the questionnaire if the data is to be so obtained?
- How will the researcher deliver the questionnaire and retrieve it when it is completed?
- How can the required informant be made to feel that he or she wants to contribute data required for the research project?

There are no simple answers to these questions but there are some guidelines which are worth following.

- If the data required can be expressed in terms of values on scales or order in a list or with answers which can be predetermined by the researcher and reduced to selecting different groups or categories, then a questionnaire can be an invaluable way of collecting data. If not then interviews or other data collecting approaches would be better. For example, a questionnaire would be excellent for collecting data about opinions which may be reduced to a scale such as the Likert Scale. But if the data requires nuanced opinions then a questionnaire will not be a successful way of collecting the required data.

- It is sometimes the case that the researcher can identify the data required, but is not clear who would be able to supply the data. In such cases interviews are probably a better way. Also if the data required is likely to be known only to senior or top managers it is probably better not to use a questionnaire. Senior and top managers can have a poor opinion of questionnaires and the data obtained from these instruments.
- Virtually all researchers are faced with the challenge of finding appropriate informants. Cold calling on individuals can result in blunt and sometimes embarrassing rejections. Many individuals have busy schedules and often they do not perceive researchers' requirements as being of import to their personal objectives. Posting questionnaires is expensive and there is a high rate of rejection, even by personal assistants or other administrative staff before the questionnaire even reaches the intended informant. e-mail is not much better as unsolicited e-mail is often perceived as span. Researchers need to locate a gatekeeper who can assist with a personal introduction to relevant informants. This approach ensures a high level of questionnaire completion. If personal contact has been made then the questionnaire delivery and retrieval issue should not be a problem.
- The issue of making the informant feel that their contribution is important is critical especially when seeking data from top and senior management. Having these people feel that they can make a difference to your research can sometimes lead to the researcher being given assistance in a variety of ways over and above that which was originally requested, However if the researcher is seen to be insincere in this respect then it is probable that the questionnaire will not be completed and no further help will be forthcoming.

Given that the above issues are clarified then the detail of questionnaire development follows.

3.4 Different types of questionnaires

Questionnaires may be categorised in a number of ways. In fact there seems to be an almost endless number of ways of describing questionnaires. As the purpose of this chapter is to describe questionnaires in academic research it is useful to focus on a few different categories. Questionnaires may be used to collect facts such as the turnover, income, number of employees, number of inventory items, the length of a product life cycle to mention only a few items. With a similar purpose a structured fact collecting questionnaire may be designed where the informant is offered both closed and open questions. An example of this is provides in Appendix 1.

A questionnaire may also be used to collect opinions such as, What will be the next important management theory which will have to be learnt by aspiring managers? Or Does your computer facilities operate with adequate reliability to be able to facilitate the achievement of your corporate objectives? Even when the primary intention is to collect opinions there will inevitable be some fact collection concerning the individual from whom the data is being collected. The questionnaire shown in Appendix 2 is an opinion based instrument.

Some questionnaires may have as their object the description of research subjects and these questionnaires may be referred to as exploratory or descriptive. Other questionnaires may be looking for data for the purposes of hypothesis testing. The questionnaire shown in Appendix 2 achieves both of these and more will be said about this later.

One more category of questionnaire is exhibited in this chapter and that is when the questionnaire becomes part of the research technique itself and this is demonstrated through the use of a Delphi Technique which is discussed later.

3.5 Questionnaire design options

There is a wide range of options available when designing a questionnaire and this allows the researcher to tailor-make a questionnaire to fit the exact requirements. The design options include the number of questions, the structure of the questions, the wording of the questions, the order of the questions, the length of the questions, the type of questions asked as well as the media used to deliver and retrieve the data.

Although questionnaires are used extensively the assumption that a questionnaire is the best option to use should not be the default position for academic research. The process of managing questionnaire based research which involves designing, creating, despatching and receiving returned questionnaires as well as coding and analysing questionnaire data is much more challenging than is often appreciated and it should not be undertaken without careful consideration of alternative approaches to data collection.

It is important to note that questionnaire development is part of the latter stages of the research design[33] and thus issues related to the purpose of the research, the research question/s, the data required, and access to this data, should all be clear in the mind of the researcher before he or she commences constructing a questionnaire.

3.6 Pre-made versus bespoke questionnaires

There is a range of questionnaires which are used in academic research and these may be categorised in a number of ways. An important distinction which is made is between pre-made versus bespoke questionnaires, which are questionnaires specifically developed by the researcher himself or herself for the research in hand. Pre-made questionnaires are those which have been used before and their function validated in earlier research studies. Where this is the case there may be more confidence that the questionnaire performs in the way that the researcher is proposing. This is what is meant by validity of the questionnaire and a previously used ques-

---

[33] Unfortunately some academic researchers make the decision to use questionnaires too early in the research design process and this may lead individuals down a difficult route.

tionnaire will have been pre-validated[34]. The advantage of using such a questionnaire is to prevent the researcher from having to re-invent the wheel and thereby reduce the amount of time, effort and cost involved in obtaining a usable questionnaire. But a previously validated questionnaire may not suit a particular research purpose and it is generally not possible to change a research agenda to match a validated questionnaire. Sometimes different parts of a number of previously validated questionnaires are re-assembled as a new questionnaire. If this is the case then the new questionnaire has to be re-validated in the same way as a completely new questionnaire. The validation process involves not only reference to the literature but also obtaining information from knowledgeable informants and perhaps a focus group discussion. Some researchers argue that before a bespoke questionnaire can be accepted it should be used on a pre-test or field test exploratory sample of some size and be examined for validity and reliability.

3.7 The range of issues needed to be considered in designing a questionnaire

Questionnaires may be used as part of an interview. Many people have been stopped in the street by a researcher who has requested "five minutes to ask a few questions" and this is frequently a questionnaire based interview. In a similar manner a researcher may present a questionnaire as the primary data collection instrument during a formal interview in the office of the informant.

In some research projects the completion of questionnaires may be undertaken by third parties such as students. When this is done it is important to be confident of the skills and the integrity of the people chosen to do this task. The researcher may feel it necessary to check with informants that their data has been correctly recorded. This cannot be done if anonymity of the informant is required.

---

[34] Of course, this should not be taken for granted and the researcher should carefully check that the questionnaire was appropriately validated before use.

A different approach is to use self completion questionnaires, where these data collection instruments are sent to prospective respondents who then complete the questionnaire on their own. In the past such questionnaires were sent by post, but today they are more likely to be e-mailed, sometimes referred to as an internet based questionnaire or placed on a web site, a web based questionnaire. A self completion questionnaire is one of the least personal ways of collecting data and normally has a low response rate. In two recent research studies response rates of 0.1% have been reported. Response rates may be improved if some sort of reward is offered to potential informants, but this also leads to problems if anonymity is required. One step that a researcher may take to improve the response is to make contact with the group of informants which he or she would like to have complete the questionnaire by phone or by e-mail. An example of such an e-mail is supplied in Exhibit 3.2 at the end of the Chapter.

It is sometimes suggested that internet or web based questionnaires have a lower response rate than the older approach i.e. postal questionnaires. This may well be true but all questionnaires which are sent to potential informants without prior agreement will have low response rates. If potential informants are contacted in advance and if they agree to participate in the research then there is a much higher chance of a good response rate.

A recent research project in which a web based questionnaire was used and potential informants were e-mailed inviting them to participate, produced an unfortunate result. Very few of the potential informants complete the questionnaire. On close inspection to was found that the spam catchers on the computers of the potential participants were not allowing the e-mailed requests to get through to the potential informants. Test runs should have been performed to check for this.

The self completion questionnaire can result in the informant answering questions which he or she does not really understand. It can also result in mischievous informants deliberately supplying inaccurate data.

3.8 Types of research

Questionnaires may be used to collect different types of data and the type of data required is determined by the nature of the research being pursued. If exploratory research[35] is being undertaken then the questions may be in the form of open questions and will tend to seek general data or general opinions in a form which will not be susceptible to inferential statistical analysis. An example of such a questionnaire is shown in Appendix 1 at the end of the Chapter. However descriptive statistical analysis[36] may be performed. Questionnaires aimed at descriptive research[37] will have a combination of open and closed questions but the objective of such a research study will still be to acquire data which will primarily not be susceptible to inferential statistical analysis. In formal or experimental or causative research the questions are designed to capture data for inferential statistical analysis, but usually some descriptive statistical analysis is also performed.

3.9 The route to a competent questionnaire

As mentioned above whether or not a questionnaire will be used in an academic research project depends on the research design. In turn the research design is function of a number of antecedent issues which include both the research topic and the research problem. Once the research problem is established specific research questions may be developed and at this point it becomes clearer

---

[35] Exploratory research is a term used to describe high level research where the parameters for the research are very broad. In exploratory research the domain may not yet be fully defined and a research question may not yet be adequately focused.

[36] Descriptive statistical analysis refers to the use of measures of central tendency and dispersion, but does not try to generalise from a sample to a population. It also employs the use of tables and graphs.

[37] Descriptive research will address more detail than exploratory research. It may employ descriptive statistical methods, but it will not attempt to be inferential.

what type of data is required. The required data is one of the most critical issues in deciding whether a questionnaire could be of value in the research design.

There are several other issues involved in compiling a questionnaire which are shown in the research model in Figure 3.1 below.

1. Field of study to be researched
2. Topic of research
3. Research problem
4. Research question
5. Research sub-questions
6. The variables, issues and constructs
7. Questionnaire questions

Figure 3.1: The steps in academic research moving from the most basic issue at the bottom

The issues in Figure 3.1 can be seen as existing at different levels and each level need completion before the next level is engaged.

There is seldom any difficulty in identifying a researcher's field of study. The only problem which can arise with this is related to the fact that most business and management researchers today undertake research in multi-disciplinary fields of study. This should not create a problem other than at doctoral level where the degree candidate would have to be properly acquainted with more than one set of literature. Where multiple sets of literature are involved the reading requirement can be heavy and also the researcher can become confused as to which literature is the more or most important.

The topic which is to be researched will be an area within the field of study with which the researcher wishes to become more expert.

The research problem is a specific issue or challenge for which a solution is sought. This is an important issue as it can determine the research methodology which is required.

The research question is a high level question which will need to be reduced to a number of more direct or focused sub-questions. Although many research projects nominally have one research question most will have a number of sub-questions and at doctoral level there may be between 4 and 8 such sub-questions. It is not unusual to find as many as 10 sub-questions, but any more than this will make the whole research considerably more difficult.

After the sub-questions have been established there needs to be a further breakdown of the questions to a level which is suitable for a questionnaire. In doing this it is necessary to carefully consider the variables, issues and constructs involved.

It is critical that the questionnaire questions are prepared with all of these many issues firmly in mind. From the above it can be seen that the production of a competent questionnaire is not a trivial task and the researcher should not rush to prepare a questionnaire without considerable preparatory thought and work. Unfortunately this advice is not always taken and researchers sometimes find themselves with many "nice-to-know" questions which are of little value and may get in the way of the main research issues.

3.10 Scales used in questionnaires

The choice of an appropriate scale is an important issue in questionnaire development. There are a number of different types of scales which may be used and the researcher needs to reflect carefully on this issue. Using a scale means that the researcher offers the informant a range of values from which he or she may select as being most appropriate to a particular question. An example of this would be *On a scale of 1 to 5 please state how satisfactory you found the customer service component of your experience, where 1 is the least satisfactory and 5 is the most satisfactory possible.*

A Likert Scale named after Rensis Likert, a founder of the University of Michigan's Institute for Social Research, is a psychometric measure frequently used in questionnaires and is the most commonly used scale in survey research. When completing a Likert scale questionnaire informants answer in levels of agreement with a statement. Each question is referred to as a Likert item, although it usually appears to be a scale of itself, and a Likert scale is the sum of a number of Likert items. Likert items may be graduated using 5, 7 or 9 positions of difference, and it is common to have an odd number of positions. The questionnaire responses can be analysed individually or summed to create a score for the group. This group score is a Likert scale, and can be treated as interval data.

Sometimes words are associated with different scores on a scale. An example of this would be the designation of a score of 1 as extremely poor performance; a score of 2 as poor performance; a score of 3 as mediocre performance; a score of 4 as good performance and a score of 5 as excellent performance. Using these words can introduce a level ambiguity in terms of what the researcher believes these words describe and how the informant might interpret them. To avoid this type of problem a scale from 1 to 5 may be used with a question which allows the informant to strongly disagree and strongly agree with a statement. An example of this is The Unit's performance was excellent; please indicate on a scale of 1 to 5 your level of disagreement or agreement, where 1 is strongly disagree and 5 is strongly agree. This approach is used in the examples in the book.

3.10.1 The granularity of the scale

Granularity refers to the range of choices offered to the informant. A scale of 1 to 10 provides a much wider range of possible answers than a 1 to 5 range. The wider the range the easier it is will to detect statistical variation in the answers. However, there is concern that the informant may not be able to distinguish between what would be meant if they indicated a score of 7 rather than a score of 8. Despite this, questionnaires are produced with scales of 12, 20 and even 41 choices.

3.10.2 Balancing the questionnaire

Questionnaires may be designed with an equal number of choices representing a positive outlook and a negative outlook, but this is not always the case. Sometimes there is an assumption that the issue being studied will mostly be considered positive, or for that matter negative, and the researcher is looking to examine fine differences in the side of the scale which is expected to have attracted the more attention. In such a case a scale could be set up on a 1 to 10 basis with only the points 1 and 2 being used to capture negative attitudes and the numbers 3 to 10 capturing positive views.

3.10.3 The odd and even number of categories issue

A questionnaire may be designed with an even or an odd number of points in the scale. For example a 2, 4, 6, or 8 point scale may be used. In this case the scale is annotated to explain that scores 2 and 4 reveal a negative attitude and scores 6 and 8 refer to a positive feeling about the subject of the research. This structure is used so that an informant cannot easily avoid expressing either a positive or negative attitude. A neutral position is not accommodated by this type of scale. This situation is sometimes referred to as a forcing scale. On the other hand, with a 3, 5 or 7 point scale it is possible to have a mid-point which may give the informant the opportunity to offer a neutral response.

3.11 Working through the questionnaire preparatory issues

The following is a worked example of the building of a questionnaire. This work should be undertaken as part of a research questionnaire protocol which is shown in Exhibit 3.1 at the end of the Chapter. Protocols are an intrinsic part of research because they require researchers to think through the issues that have to be addressed if the research is to be successful. Some researchers see the research protocol as being a type of project plan which is presented in the form of a list of things that have to be done. As such it is worth spending time on producing a comprehensive list, but even with a thoroughly worked out protocol the research may still run into difficulties.

3.12 Example of Questionnaire Preparation

The **field of study** to be addressed is **Information systems management**, which is an eclectic area that draws on a number of different traditional disciplines including operations, finance, marketing, human resources and operations research. This field is well established as being multidisciplinary in nature.

The **topic** which this research will address is that of **How e-Government investment may be evaluated**. Before the topic could have been established it would have been necessary for the researcher to have familiarised himself or herself with the literature in this field[38].

The research problem is that with tighter restrictions on government funding the Treasury wish to understand how e-Government applications investment can be assessed for its effectiveness.

It is important to make clear at this stage that before a researcher can proceed with a research question it would be essential for him or her to have acquired a detailed knowledge of the topic and the research problem. This detailed knowledge could be the result of some prior exploratory research, or it could be the result of the researcher's employment experiences supported or underpinned by a literature review. To obtain this level of contextual knowledge the researcher may have already undertaken some preliminary interviews or even held a focus group. But whatever the source some detailed knowledge needs to be in place in order to proceed to the next step.

The research question is:-

How can the investment employed in developing and operating e-Government applications be assessed for its effectiveness?

The research question cannot be answered directly as it is too high level to facilitate close examination[39]. It therefore needs to be reduced to a series of sub-questions.

---

[38] At doctoral level the researcher is required to have also read a material amount in related fields as well.

[39] Not all researchers would agree with this. Post-modernists and other relativists would argue that creating a list of sub-questions is a reductionist approach which

The **research sub-questions** related to this research questionnaire are:-

1. Who identifies e-Government application requests and what process is used to appraise an application?
2. How is the amount of capital funding required for e-Government applications estimated?
3. How are the intended benefits identified and what criteria are used to assess their effectiveness?
4. How are the amount of operating costs and new benefits required from e-Government applications estimated?
5. Which person or committee decides on the viability of the e-Government application and which technique/s are used in doing this?
6. What are the organisation's criteria for declaring an e-Government application to be effective?
    a. Have standards been established and accepted by decision makers as investment targets or benchmarks?
    b. Is there adequate historic data available to make a before and after comparison?

Creating the list of sub-questions is one of the more creative aspects of questionnaire design[40]. Careful thought needs to be given to these questions as they have to be answerable in such a way that they will shed light on the main research question. Here the most common error is to create too many sub-questions. It is worthwhile to repeat the advice given above that more than about 8 sub-questions will cause the research project to be quite onerous.

---

sometimes distorts the "real" issues when studying organisations. For this reason these types of researchers would not be inclined to use a questionnaire as an approach to data collection. The influence of Relativism has increased in Business and Management Studies in recent years.

[40] Such a list as this is not likely to be definitive. There are many other questions of interest to other researchers and the researcher needs to be clear on the issues that are really of interest to him or to her.

3.13 Building the questionnaire items

These sub-questions are now in sufficient detail to provide the next step of identifying issues or variables or constructs. This process is sometimes referred to as unpacking the sub-questions to create the questionnaire questions required.

Looking at these questions closely they contain words like Who, How and What. These simple common every day words, who, how and what tend to camouflage the complexity within them and they have to be converted into more direct and easier to answer questions which may be placed in a questionnaire.

It is worth emphasising the fact that an important aspect of this type of questionnaire building is that different researchers will look at this list of sub-questions and will see different issues or variables or constructs or will at least give different levels of importance to the issues or variables or constructs contained therein. This is where the researchers' creativity comes into play and it is important not to rush this part of questionnaire development. Without adequate creativity a questionnaire will become nothing more than a number or data collecting activity which will not lead to insightful research. In this example the researcher wants to be able to comment on the **details** of the processes, practices and people involved in the evaluation of e-Government investment and thus a qualitative approach will be required. If on the other hand a more aggregated knowledge of these processes is required, say, for the purposes of comparison, then a quantitative approach would have been needed. Aggregated results are more effective if the researcher wishes to compare one government division to another and for this type of work a quantitative approach would be preferable.

From the above research questions the following variables can be identified:-

1. In sub-question 1 the emphasis is on ***who*** and in this respect the role or the function of the person is required instead of the name of an individual.

2. In sub-question 2 the emphasis is on ***how*** and in this case an activity or even a process is being sought.
3. In sub-question 3 there are two parts and these are a ***how*** question and a ***what*** question. The how question may be a process but it is one for which there is likely to be a model used by the organisation. The ***what*** question is looking for a set of rules. Both of these questions may also involve identifying processes.
4. In sub-question 4 the emphasis is on **how** and this refers to a process.
5. In sub-question 5 the emphasis is **which** and this refers to the entities and techniques that are required.
6. In sub-question 6 the emphasis is **what** and this refers to standards within the organisation.

    a. Have standards been established and accepted by decision makers as investment targets or benchmarks?

    b. Is there adequate historic data available to make a before and after comparison?

It is useful to present this information in a table as shown below in Figure 3.2:-

	Sub-question	Focus	Data collection approach	Quantitative/ Qualitative
1	**Who** identifies e-Government application requests and what process is used to appraise an application?	Who & What	A questionnaire could be used to collect such data. Whether a questionnaire is used would depend on how many informants are required and how much variability is expected in the answers.	Either a quantitative or a qualitative approach could be used especially if there are different ranges of data.
2	**How** is the amount of capital funding required for e-Government applications estimated?	How	A list of capital funding estimating techniques could be produced and informants asked to indicate their view by ticking a box or supplying an alternative approach.	Similar to the above

	Sub-question	Focus	Data collection approach	Quantitative/ Qualitative
3	**How** are the intended benefits identified and **what** criteria are used to assess their effectiveness?	How & What	There may be several different approaches to identifying benefits and the researcher may wish to ask the informant for an opinion on how this is done in their organization.	Similar to the above
4	**How** are the amount of operating costs and new benefits required from e-Government applications estimated?	How	Similar to the above	Similar to the above
5	**Which** person or committee decides on the viability of the e-Government application and which technique/s are used in doing this?	Which	Similar to the above	Similar to the above
6	**What** are the organisation's criteria for declaring an e-Government application to be effective? Have standards been established and accepted by decision makers as investment targets or benchmarks? Is there adequate historic data available to make a before and after comparison?	What	Similar to the above	Similar to the above

Figure 3.2: Unpacking the research questions

3.14 Constructing the questionnaire

The next step in the questionnaire development process is to begin the creation the questionnaire questions.

In order to obtain a full understanding of the situation the first sub-question, ***Who identifies e-Government application requests and what process is used?*** may require several questions in the questionnaire. Before describing the actual questions it is important to make the distinction between closed and open questions. A closed question offers the informant a number of choices to choose from. The simplest of closed questions is,

Tick the word corresponding to your gender? Male Female

or

Circle the option that describes you: I am employed Full time Part time

An open question does not offer predetermined choices. Thus the same question would be

What gender are you? ________________________________

Returning to the first sub-question ***Who identifies e-Government application requests and what process is used to appraise an application?*** and taking a descriptive approach, it may be appropriate to ask, inter alia:-

Is there an individual in your Department who is responsible for indentifying e-Government requests? Yes No

If your answer is No, go directly to question 18.

If your answer is Yes, what is the title of the post?

____

Who are the primary decision makers when evaluating such requests?

How many decision makers are there in total?

Are the same people from these roles always involved?

Are the decision makers required to consult advisors?

Now there are four questions required to obtain a rounded understanding of the answer to the first part of sub-question 1 which are:

Who are the primary decision makers? Tick as appropriate.

Chief financial Officer ____

Chief Accountant ____

Consultants ____

Others please specify ________________

This type of question is sometimes referred to as a multiple choice question as the main answers have been anticipated. The fourth choice opens this question and the informant may then provide a more complicated answer.

How many decision makers are there in total? ____________________

Are the same people from these roles always involved?______________

Are the decision makers required to consult advisors? Yes No

This Yes or No type question is sometimes called a dichotomous question. Looking at the second half of the first sub-question, there might also be multiple questions in the questionnaire, such as:

Do you use a standard computer program? Yes No

If Yes, what is it called? ______________________________________

What types of calculation are performed? (tick all that apply)

Payback _____

NPV _____

IRR _____

PI _____

Other please specify ____________________

How much time do you normally have to make such a decision[41]?

____

How important is the proposed system champion in the evaluation process?

____

[41] This question could be answered quantitatively i.e. 5 hours or it could be answered qualitatively *We do not often have much time*. Some researchers would prefer not allow this type of ambiguity and convert the question to only allow a tick the box type answer.

Using this approach all the other research sub-questions are expanded and prepared in such a way that an informant completing a questionnaire can offer his or her understanding of the situation.

The list of the issues contained in sub-questions can be substantial and 30 to 50 questionnaire questions[42] will easily be generated.

It is critical that each individual question in the questionnaire is capable of being mapped onto the research sub-question. As may be seen from the above description usually several questionnaire questions will be required for a sub-question. In the above example four questionnaire questions were used to answer the first part of the first sub-question and then the researcher needs to decide how the captured data should be analysed to produce a useable understanding of the answer to this one sub-question. This calls on the creativity of the researcher.

It is important to remember that the greater the number of questions in a questionnaire the less likely it is that informants will attempt to complete it. Perhaps even more problematic is the fact that the questions towards the end of a long questionnaire are sometimes skipped over in haste and are thus answered without proper attention to what might be the most appropriate answer or are sometimes just left unanswered. It is not possible to suggest an ideal number of questions as all research projects will have different environments and require different data sets but questionnaires which exceed more than 10 pages or 10 computer screens will generally be considered long by potential informants. This size issue can also be seen in terms of the length of time to complete the questionnaire. If the questionnaire needs more than 15 minutes to complete then there will be fewer individuals who will want to make that amount of time available to the researcher.

In addition to the number of questions the way the questionnaire is structured is also an important issue. A questionnaire should, wher-

[42] Some researchers refer to questionnaire questions as questionnaire items.

ever possible, be divided into separate sections or parts. This helps the informant feel that he or she is making progress by completing a number of sections. In Appendix 1 and 2 the questions provided are examples of this approach. Note that a 9 point Likert type scale is used here.

3.15 Pre-coded questions

When completed questionnaires are being prepared for entry into a computer, the answers to questions may have to be coded so that they can be processed by the software available on the computer. Of course if the answer to a question is a number this could be entered directly. The process of coding is not difficult although it can be time consuming and mistakes can be made. To speed up the coding procedures a series of pre-codes may be used. Pre-codes will be values which are previously attributed to different possible answers to a question. For example with the question:-

Tick the word corresponding to your gender Male Female

The reply Male could be pre-coded 1 and the reply Female could be pre-coded 2. In a similar way the question,

Are the decision makers required to consult advisors? Yes No

This question might have the answer Yes pre-coded as 1 and the answer No pre-coded as 2. Of course, more complicated pre-coding is required for more sophisticated questions and their answers.

There is a substantial amount published on the subject of coding questionnaires when they have been returned to the researcher. However this topic more correctly falls under the subject of processing the data from the questions.

3.16 Continuing building the questionnaire

In this way the questionnaire is built up to collect the data required to answer the research sub-questions and thus ultimately the main research question. Some data will naturally be expressed numerically such as age, salary[43], the number of widgets produced or sold. However other data will relate to issues which are not so obviously numerical such as ***How successful was the implementation of the Information System?*** To capture an answer to this question in a useful way, a scale has to be established which can be used in the process of "measuring" the issues or variables. Researchers sometimes use a Likert type scale[44] for such purposes. The Likert scale may be used to ask the informant to indicate on a scale of 1 to 5 or 1 to 7 or even 1 to 9 the level of agreement he or she has with a given proposition. An example of this is shown in Figure 3.3.

	Strongly Disagree / Strongly Agree
In our organisation Chief Financial Officers use Payback Techniques when preparing investment plans	1___ 2___ 3___ 4___ 5___ 6___ 7

Figure 3.3: A Likert scale with a 1 to 7 range

The work involved in deciding on which scale to use in building a questionnaire is an important part of the questionnaire design and requires a careful understanding of how the results of the research will be used.

---

43 As a general rule an informant's age and salary should not be requested directly. It is more common to ask an informant to indicate the range of ages in which he or she falls. A similar approach is usually taken to salary.

44 A Likert Scale named after Rensis Likert, a founder of the University of Michigan's Institute for Social Research, is a psychometric measure frequently used in questionnaires and is the most commonly used scale in survey research. When completing a Likert scale questionnaire participants answer in levels of agreement with a statement. Each question is referred to as a Likert item, although it usually appears to be a scale of itself, and a Likert scale is the sum of a number of Likert items. With Likert scales it is common to have an odd number of positions. The mid-position is regarded as neither supporting nor disagreeing with the proposition. Sometimes a forced opinion is gained by removing the mid-position. The informant can be analysed individually or summed to create a score for the group. This group score is a Likert scale, and can be treated as interval data.

3.17 Moving to hypothesis testing

Up to this point the questionnaire which has been developed is suitable for either explorative or descriptive research, but not for formal hypothesis testing research. An hypothesis is a claim made by a researcher which he or she tries to reject. If the data obtained does not allow the hypothesis to be rejected then the claim remains and is "accepted" for the time being. In formal hypothesis testing research an hypothesis needs to be stated in such a way that it can be rejected. Form the work done in an earlier data collection exercise it might be discovered that either Chief Financial Officers or Financial Accountants are responsible for producing e-Government financial investment plans. It might also appear from initial research that Payback techniques are the most likely to be used and NPV techniques are the second most likely to be used for this purpose.

If this is the case then it is possible to test these claims by stating a Null Hypothesis (described as $\mathbf{H_0}$) which is a claim that will be tested with the view of rejection:

($\mathbf{H_0}$) = Chief Financial Officers use Payback Techniques when preparing investment plans.

And the alternative Hypothesis (which is always described as $\mathbf{H_1}$):

($\mathbf{H_1}$) = Financial Accountants do not use Payback Techniques when preparing investment plans.

The questionnaire questions could then be:-

Chief Financial Officers use Payback Techniques when preparing investment plans — Yes — No

and

Chief Financial Accountants use Payback Techniques when preparing investment plans — Yes — No

If this first suggestion is used then the hypothesis can be tested using the Chi-Square technique which employs counts of the Yes and the No answers.

A similar question could be posed using a Likert type scale and then a more traditional hypothesis test may be used employing a mean and standard error approach.

3.18 Other parts of the questionnaire

The above section describes how to create questions which will constitute the main body of the questionnaire. In addition it is necessary to write an introduction to the questionnaire explaining what its objectives are, the different parts of the questionnaire, how it should be completed, the time it will take to complete and inviting informants to complete it. This section should also indicate who is responsible for the research and how to contact him or her. The tone of the questionnaire is set in this section as is its creditability with the prospective informant. Thus the introduction is of critical importance as it is on reading this that the informant will decide on whether to continue and complete the answers required. The work involved in this part of the questionnaire should not be rushed. Figure 3.4 is an example of the Opening page of a questionnaire.

This research is being conducted under the auspices of the University of the Far North Western Plains. This research instrument has been presented to the university's ethics committee and was approved by them on Friday 25, January 20XX. If you have any questions concerning this please contact me at the e-mail address below.

The following questionnaire has been designed to help assess the effectiveness of the corporate information systems used to support the firm in achieving its objectives. This user satisfaction approach to measuring the effectiveness of information systems is used extensively in businesses throughout the world.

This questionnaire has been divided into four parts.

Part A relates to personal details about your position in the firm.

Parts B and C use the same set of 35 statements but answered through two different perspectives.

Part D contains one specific question as well as an opportunity for you to provide open-ended comment on the systems.

Your responses to the statements in Part B refer to your expectations, given an ideal situation, of your firm's information systems. Your answers to the second set of 35 questions in Part C refer to how the Information Systems Department of the firm actually performs in terms of these systems attributes. Finally, in Part D we would like you to rate your overall opinion of the information systems, and we would welcome any comments that you would like to make concerning your own experience with the Information Systems Department in respect of its effectiveness. The questionnaire uses a nine-point scale where 1 means you Strongly disagree and 9 means you Strongly agree. For each statement please tick the number that corresponds to your level of agreement. Please do not tick or circle between the numbers.

For example, if you agree quite strongly with the statement '*I expect ease of access to computer facilities*' your rating in the first set of statements could be:

Strongly Disagree 1 ☐ 2☐ 3☐ 4☐ 5 ☐ 6 ☐ 7☐ 8☐✓9☐ Strongly agree

If you do not feel that the performance of the Information Systems Department in actually providing these facilities is particularly good, your rating in the second set of statements might be:

Strongly Disagree 1 ☐ 2☐ 3☐✓ 4☐ 5 ☐ 6 ☐ 7☐ 8☐9☐ Strongly agree

Please rate all statements and tick one and only one response.

The questionnaire should not take more than 15-20 minutes to complete. All information supplied by respondents will be treated with the utmost confidence. Your views will only be reported in summary. The data will be stored securely until the research project has been completed at which point the questionnaires will be shredded and the computer files deleted. Thank you very much for your assistance in this research. Please return your completed questionnaire to the survey administrator.

Professor Dan Remenyi
IT Effectiveness Assessment Services
dan.remenyi@gmail.com

Figure 3.4: A sample of an opening page for a questionnaire

In addition asking question of the sort described above may cause the data so collected to fall within the ambit of the Data Protection Act. Universities take the provisions of the Data protection Act seriously as if there are infringements of this act universities can be fined and these fines can be substantial[45].

Traditionally the personal questions were located at the front end of the questionnaire immediately behind the introduction, however it is now increasingly common to see them placed on at the end of the questionnaire. It is argued that the informant will want to get into the main questions as soon as possible and to ask him or her for their personal details may distract them and they may change their minds and not participate in the research.

3.19 Personal details about the informant

It is sometimes necessary to obtain some information about the personal details of the informant. This is referred to as demographic details although this is not exactly the correct usage of the word demographic as it refers to a population. When the personal details are summarised they could be referred to as demographic information. Knowing the informant's role title, division in which employed, and length of service with the organisation may be useful to enhance the analysis of the data. However there is a general tendency to seek too much of this type of data and every question under this section should be carefully justified. It is important to be aware that informants may not wish to indicate their age, their gender, their religious affiliation, the state of their health, marital status, national origin, or their salary grade as they may regard such questions as an intrusion into their privacy[46]. Thus these questions should only be asked if they are essential to the research.

---

[45] http://www.recordsmanagement.ed.ac.uk/InfoStaff/DPstaff/DP_Research/ResearchAndDPA.htm

[46] In certain part s of the world asking such questions may be illegal. http://www.dummies.com/how-to/content/illegal-and-inappropriate-interview-questions.html

3.20 Common vocabulary

An issue in building a questionnaire is that the researcher has to make sure that he or she is using a common vocabulary with the informant. The researcher needs to minimise the use of jargon and other words which may not be familiar to the informants. It is important not to use acronyms unless it is clear that any informant will understand them. Acronyms always need to be explained by using the full words first followed by the abbreviation in brackets. Of course words which will be known to informants need not be explained. For example a questionnaire which will be sent to computer users will most probably not need an explanation of the term acronym IS.

The questions should not be long winded. The structure of the question should not be complex and the use of "and" or "or" should be minimised.

The language of the questions needs to be relatively simple. Some researchers advocate supplying a short glossary of terms at the end of the questionnaire, but others suggest that if this is needed one or more questions are too complex.

3.21 The nature of open questions

It is sometimes suggested that open questions can be a bridge between the questionnaire and the interview method of collecting data because the open question allows the informant to write whatever he or she wishes. In principle the open question tries to reach beyond the limited confines of a simple list of questions as it tries to tap a more detailed insight as to what the informant feels about the subject being researched. But there is the inherent contradiction here in that a questionnaire offers a relatively quick and easy way for an informant to contribute to a research project until open questions are used. Open questions can take much time and concentration if the informant is to answer them competently.

In practice only a relatively small number of informants offer more than one or two words as a reply to open questions and thus although they may produce more data than closed questions they generally do not produce anything like the data which is obtainable from an interview.

Open questions can offer a challenge with regards to coding and the researcher has to pre-arrange the codes which will be used for different data produced by these questions.

3.22 Screening questions

Sometimes the researcher will only require informants to complete certain parts of the questionnaire if they give a particular answer to a screening question. An example of this is that the researcher may only want a set of questions answered by informants who have a particular type of experience. The question which will determine this is referred to as a screening question and an example of this is:-

If you have had face-to-face contact with complaining customers answer the next 5 questions. If not go to question no 30.

Screening questions are important as the researcher certainly does not want an informant to attempt to answer questions of which they have no experience.

The software packages available with which to develop a questionnaire handle these sorts of screening questions well.

3.23 Layout of the questionnaire

The layout of a questionnaire is of considerable importance. If the questionnaire is laid out attractively and in an easy to read and easy to reply to manner there will be a higher response rate. Here are some of the rules which should be applied.

If the questionnaire has different sections as many do, then these should be clear to the informant. Sometimes different colours can be helpful in distinguishing different sections from one another. Questions should be numbered clearly and simply. Roman numerals should not be used. A reasonable amount of space should be left between questions. When open questions are used there should be adequate space of a reply.

With closed questions, not too many options should be given. Generally no more than 6 to 8 is a useful rule to follow.

Where "Don't Know" or "not applicable" is a possible answer in a closed question then a provision should be made for such a reply.

3.24 Incentives for responding

It is sometimes suggested that an incentive for responding would increase the completion and return rate of questionnaires. However there are a number of problems with this idea. First of all there is the fact that many academic researchers do not have the funds to pay informants. Even a modest sum per person adds up to a large sum if it has to be offered and paid to, say, 100 informants.

In addition there is a school of thought that if a financial incentive is offered informants may regard the completion of the questionnaire as a chore for which money is paid and lose focus on the purpose of the study. It is sometimes said that a payment might impact on the informant's sense of integrity in completing the questionnaire. Clearly there is no universal agreement among academic researchers about this issue.

The same principle is sometimes applied to the offering of a lottery type of prize which will be drawn from the names of those who have completed the questionnaire.

3.25 Field testing a questionnaire

In developing a questionnaire there is a tendency for the researcher to become so close to the issues that sometimes the meaning of questions produced will not be clear to informants. For this reason it is important for all questionnaires to be field tested. The term field test is equivalent to the older term piloting but it conveys the fact that the people with whom the questionnaire should be tested should be similar to those who will be offered the questionnaire in the field. The field test should be conducted on a small sample and the actual number will depend on how big the eventual sample will be, but 4 to 8 individuals are generally considered to be enough. Before field testing it is advisable to pre-test the questionnaire.

Here 2 or 3 people will suffice and these people could be colleagues in the department. With both the pre-test and the field test it is important that the researcher takes the suggestions made by the respondents into account.

3.26 Different languages

Sometimes researchers wish to compare situations in two or more different countries. If different languages are involved the researcher will need to have a highly experienced translator convert the questionnaire to the other language. The word "convert" is used here because a simple translation may not be adequate to capture the nuances which are sometimes involved in the questions. Once the questionnaire exists in the other language then the researchers should have it reconverted by another language and research specialist back into the original language which for the purposes of this book will probably be English.

3.27 Questionnaire and Informed Consent

There is an issue of how informed consent may be acquired when an anonymous questionnaire is used. When such an instrument is used it should state that the informant is aware and agrees that by completing the questionnaire he or she is granting the researcher permission to use the data for the purposes set out in the document.

3.28 Generic issues with questionnaires

There is of course much more to be said about questionnaire design than what has been addressed above. Specialist texts are available and these should be explored carefully. In general it should be noted that using questionnaires to collect data is a much more difficult task than most researchers realise. It is intellectually challenging and it requires considerable effort. The following is a list of issues which the researcher needs to keep in mind when producing a questionnaire.

1. The response rate for questionnaires can be low and thus obtaining a usable sample size can be problematic.

2. The more questions asked the fewer questionnaires will be returned.
3. The more complex the question the more unanswered questions there will be in the returned questionnaire.
4. Some returned questionnaires will have incomplete questions or questions answered in such a way that the data cannot be used.
5. Questionnaires are not always correctly answered, i.e. respondents can lie in a questionnaire.
6. Mistakes can be made in transferring data from the questionnaire to the software package used to analyse the results.
7. Pre-coding the questionnaire can be a considerable time saver when it comes to data transfer.
8. Data validation should be performed diligently.
9. Version control of the data is essential.
10. Questionnaire data cannot be as rich as data obtained from interviewing.
11. Questionnaires require approval from the ethics committee.
12. Finding an appropriate group who will complete your questionnaire can be challenging.

There are other issues and questions which should be considered and some of these are listed below.

1. A reasonable number of responses and questions are required. With under 30 responses the value of the questionnaire is likely to be low and with less than 12 questions in the questionnaire it may not be worthwhile to collect the data. There will be other numeric constraints depending on the type of analysis which the researcher intends to perform.
2. Data entry and validation can sometimes be outsourced.
3. How should incomplete questionnaires be handled to make it acceptable to include them in the survey? Informants who have not completed all the questions could be approached to fill out the questionnaire properly.

4. A Letter of Consent will be required when using a questionnaire if the respondent's name is known. An example is shown in Exhibit 3.4.
5. Telephone questionnaire completion is acceptable but is not as effective as face-to-face questionnaire completion.
6. When acquiring data by telephone questionnaire completion it is possible to improve the questionnaire from one interview to the next but this will lead to issues of validity.
7. The cost of using questionnaires is sometimes over looked.
8. Questionnaires alone would not be considered as an adequate means of obtaining a rich picture with which to answer an academic research question. Supplementary data will be required.

3.29 Specific questionnaire types

The issues discussed above apply to questionnaires in a general sense. However, there are many specialist types of questionnaires that can be used in academic research. In this chapter two of these will be discussed and these are ServQual and Delphi Study Questionnaires. These questionnaires need to be constructed in terms of the framework which is being used. Although it is clear that these two techniques use questionnaires some researchers would argue that they should be considered under the title of different research techniques rather than being described in a chapter on questionnaires.

3.30 ServQual Questionnaires

The concept of ServQual is based on the notion that satisfaction may be measured by the difference between expectations and performance. Thus if a service or product has a higher performance rating than its expectation rating it may be said that the users of this service or product are more than satisfied. If on the other hand the expectation ratings are higher than the performance rating then it may be said that the users are not satisfied. If the expectations and performance ratings are the same then the users are satisfied. Appendix 2 at the end of the Chapter shows a questionnaire which has been set up to measure this type of concept. In Appendix 2 user satisfaction with the ICT made available to them is being measured and being used as a surrogate measure of IS Effectiveness and thus the respondents are being asked questions about their expectations and the performance of the IS function. Note that because of the need to compare expectation with performance the same set of questions is put to each informant two times. In the analysis of the data captured in this way the performance scores are subtracted from the expected scores for each variable. In this way the researcher may comment on each variable and thus identify the source of any dissatisfaction there may be among the users. This questionnaire allows for a considerable amount of analysis besides the gap analysis described above.

There is one other important point illustrated in this questionnaire. The final question is a general control question which asked the respondents to evaluate the ICT service as a whole. The previous questions addressed specific issues and this last question is used to confirm that the summation of the individual findings are at least to some extent synchronised with the generalisation which is inherent in the last question.

Finally the questionnaire leaves some space for the informants to make general comments about the provision of IS services. This is a useful attribute of a questionnaire as it allows informants to raise issues which the researcher had not incorporated formally in the list of questions.

3.31 Delphi Study Questionnaires

A Delphi Study questionnaire is shown in Appendix 3. A 9 point Likert type scales is again used here. A Delphi Study employs a highly structured questionnaire in which the informants are asked to rate the importance of a series of issues. The informants are asked to do this over 3 rounds of the questionnaire.

As the name implies a Delphi Study explores future trends or more precisely the opinion of experts about future trends. Thus Delphi

Study informants should be well informed about the topic of the study. It is important that the study begins with approximately 20 informants as these studies always incur a high level of attrition. It is desirable that round three should have at least 12 informants.

At the end of the first round the scores for each of the issues are entered into a computer and the average score and a standard deviation for each question is calculated. A second questionnaire is produced with identical questions and the informants are asked to again rate the issues being studied, but on this occasion in the light of the average scores and standard deviation of the first round of answers. The objective of this is to see if the informants will change their scores when they see the results of the first round.

Usually there will be some convergence of opinions reflected in the second round scores.

With a Delphi Study a third round is required which using the average and the standard deviation of round two asked the informants for the last time if they wish to change their scores. Again there is often some convergence of opinions.

3.32 Reliability and validity

An important issue related to a measuring instrument in academic research is its reliability and validity. The reliability of an instrument addresses the question of whether the instrument, in this case the questionnaire, will produce consistent results if it is re-used. This will be a function of the clarity of the questions and the removal of any ambiguity in the way the questions are worded. In business and management studies reliability needs to be seen in terms of the context in which the questionnaire is used. An academic researcher who uses the same questionnaire in different contexts, such as industry groups, different socio-economic groups, and different employee categories can expect to obtain different results with the same questionnaire. External factors such as the economic cycle, the political climate of the day, the attitude of the informants' employer can directly affect the outcome of a questionnaire based study. As a consequence a researcher should not expect too much from a questionnaire on the dimension of reliability.

Statisticians use Cronbach's α (alpha) as a measure of reliability. This measures the internal consistency of the data supplied. But eventually the reliability of a questionnaire will only become clear with repetitive use.

The issue of validity is also critical. Validity refers to whether the researcher is actually measuring the variable or construct which he or she thinks is being addressed. A way of thinking about this is How confident is the researcher that the informant is interpreting the question in the required way? Also there is the question of whether the variables which are used to form a construct are actually the most appropriate to group together in this way. There are a number of dimensions to validity which may be examined in different ways. There is external and internal validity. There is ex-ante and ex-post validity. There is construct and convergent validity to mention only a few dimensions of this issue. One of the ways in which a researcher can improve his or her claim for validity is to look for other sources of evidence which will support the findings of the questionnaire. The researcher could also include an open question at the end of the questionnaire. For example, such a question could say something like, "*This questionnaire has been designed for examining strategic corporate behaviour. If you have any suggestions on improving the focus of the instrument please feel free to comment*".

3.33 Software to develop a questionnaire

The list below provides names of software which is available on the web for the development of questionnaires[47]. These pieces of software regard themselves as being free although to acquire the full functionality of the program it may be necessary to purchase a fuller version of the product.

---

[47] This list was found at http://thatsblog.com/blog-tools-utilities/list-of-free-survey-tools on July 10, 2011

1. Survey Monkey[48]: Intelligent survey software for primates of all species. SurveyMonkey has a single purpose: to enable anyone to create professional online surveys quickly and easily.
2. Survey Gizmo: SurveyGizmo is a creative platform for your marketing, lead generation and research projects. Create surveys, landing pages, polls, quizzes, contact forms, ticketing queues and mobile marketing campaigns. Whatever data you need, we can help you get it.
3. Freeonlinesurveys: Create your own Free Survey in Under 10 Minutes.
4. Forecast: Forecast surveys allow you to design online surveys, collect responses from the visitors of your blog or website, analyze them and finally present the survey results – all using only your web browser and for free.
5. LimeSurvey: Open source survey tool.
6. VT Survey: VT Survey is a web-based tool which enables end users to autonomously create and run online surveys, feedback or registration forms. By providing a forms-based visual editor, the use of VTSurvey requires no programming knowledge or skills in HTML.
7. Smart Survey: Smart-Survey is an Online Survey Software Tool designed to help users create and publish custom surveys in minutes, then view results graphically and in real time.
8. Cool Surveys: Your web visitors can now participate in your own customized online survey question with answers! Our convenient survey creation wizard will automatically set up your own survey question with answers – you just cut and paste the html code and place it in your web site! Within minutes, you will have your own interactive online CoolSurvey!

---

[48] All the software products and services mentioned here are registered trademarks of their respective owners.

9. Zap Survey: Create online surveys quickly and easily using just a web browser. Send and track survey invitations all from within ZapSurvey. Interpret survey results in real-time.
10. Feedbackfarm: Unlimited survey responses per month, Customize look and feel of studies, Integrate into your site or blog.
11. Mysurveylab: 18 questions to chose from, Survey progress bar, Multi language support, Advanced collection options.
12. Instantsurvey: InstantSurvey Basic empowers anyone to quickly conduct their own online survey research.
13. Surveymethods: Create free surveys with the basic package.
14. Google Docs: Google also provides an easy to use questionnaire development tool/service.

In addition to the above there is a questionnaire design section in Google and this is accessed through docs.google.com. This allows a web based questionnaire to be developed easily and quickly. Using this technology the researcher has only to e-mail potential informant and invite them to visit the questionnaire website.

In general the questionnaire development tools available on the web are impressive and some of them continue to add further functionality. An academic should consider the use of these tools as they can reduce the amount of work in questionnaire design and questionnaire distribution. Some of the products also offer a competent level of data analysis and where thus is not enough an output file may be acquired to allow transfer to a dedicated statistical analysis program.

3.34 Software for data analysis

This chapter does not deal with data analysis. However before a questionnaire is despatched to informants the researcher should have consulted a statistics specialist as to how the data which can be collected with the questionnaire can be analysed. It is a mistake to collect the data and then seek statistical suggestions as to how it may be understood. It is always better to consult a statistician before the questionnaire design is completed. When the data has been collected without statistical advice, frequently the researcher is told that the data is not suitable for the type of analysis which would be helpful in understanding the research question and obtaining a useful answer.

3.35 Digital data

The data acquired by most questionnaires requires some processing with a computer. Sometimes sophisticated analysis using statistical software such as SPSS may be required. On other occasions a spreadsheet such as Excel may suffice. In either case provision needs to be made to enter the data and to perform checks on it to ensure it has been correctly entered. This can be a challenging process and it can require a considerable amount of time. As data entry may be performed over time version control is important.

When the data entry starts, so too should the processes of backing up the data on the computer. This requires a complete copy of the data to be held on a different storage device and that this device be situated at a different location to the original data. Researchers regularly lose data and this causes considerable delays. At least one copy of the data should be taken every time new records are added as well as an additional copy taken each week and held in a another location[49]. This will ensure that if there is a major computer catastrophe the researcher will be able to recover his or her position without too much inconvenience.

3.36 Summary

It is relatively easy to compile a questionnaire and to distribute it. Of course whether the questionnaire is valid and will lead to the acquisition of useful data is another issue. In the section above some indication is given as to the work involved in unpacking a research question to discover the elements which can be used in a question-

---

[49] Copying the data and leaving it in the office or study of the researcher does not give protection in the event of a fire or a serious flood. Carrying a copy of the data around in a pocket or in a computer bag is also quite problematic as many researchers have found.

naire and reference has been made to the issue of scales. If the researcher uses a bespoke questionnaire then he or she has to validate it. This requires the researcher to show that he or she has been able to understand the main issues around the questions asked in the questionnaire. This can be accomplished by using a focus group as well as some in depth interviews with knowledgeable informants in the topic of study. The researcher should not take it for granted that a particular question will access the data that is intended. The researcher needs to have support for this claim. If a premade questionnaire is used then the researcher has to demonstrate that he or she is familiar with the literature on the previous use of the questionnaire. Sometimes a researcher will want to use a combination of a premade questionnaire with some new questions. In such a case the questionnaire will have to be put through some degree of validation which may require a focus group and interviews.

In the past questionnaires were normally printed and distributed by postal services. This is increasingly expensive and the response rate obtained from postal distribution of a questionnaire is generally not good. To reduce costs, questionnaires have been designed as electronic documents and distributed by e-mail. Today questionnaires are placed on the Web and the sample frame is e-mailed requesting individuals to participate in the study. These e-mail and web innovations have not necessarily produced much better response rates. Unsolicited e-mails are normally considered spam and are often not even read. What seems to be the case is that a reasonable questionnaire response will only be obtained if the researcher has made advanced arrangements with specific potential informants. This used to mean that the researcher would write to a desired informant and request that the questionnaire be completed. If there was a positive reply the questionnaire was then despatched. The same principle of approaching the informant in advance is still applicable today. The other approach to attempting to obtain a high response rate is for the researcher to request an interview with the informant. Here the researcher completes the questionnaire in the company of the informant. This approach is sometimes referred to as structured interviewing.

3.37 End Note

To conclude here are the 10 principles for making questionnaires effective for academic research.

1. Carefully plan all aspects of the questionnaire using the questionnaire protocol provided at the end of this Chapter.
2. Be realistic about how many questions should be asked and the likely completion rate.
3. Remember that not all questionnaires that have been completed and returned will be useable.
4. Make sure that advice concerning the analysis has been taken from an appropriate statistician.
5. Do not under-estimate the work involved in the data management aspects of using a questionnaire. Keeping backups of data is essential.
6. Comply with the rules of questionnaire design.
7. Include in the questionnaire the fact that ethics approval has been obtained. State how this approval was obtained and the date thereof. In addition you may also need to obtain a signed Letter of Informed Consent from each informant.
8. Prepare a reminder letter or e-mail to be sent after the date which was required for the return of the data. One reminder is adequate.
9. Close the data collection and begin with the pre-processing validation of the data.
10. Proceed with the data analysis.

Exhibits for Chapter Three

Exhibit 3.1: Example of a Questionnaire Protocol

Item	Issue	Detail	Notes
1	Research Topic	e-Government application evaluation	
2	Research question	How can the investment employed in developing and operating e-Government applications be assessed for its effectiveness?	
3	Sub-questions	1. Who identifies e-Government application requests and what process is used to appraise an application? 2. How is the amount of capital funding required for e-Government applications estimated? 3. How are the intended benefits identified and what criteria are used to assess their effectiveness? 4. How are the amount of operating costs and new benefits required from e-Government applications estimated? 5. Which person or committee decides on the viability of the e-Government application and which technique/s are used in doing this? 6. What are the organisation's criteria for declaring an e-Government application to be effective?	
4	Informant/s	Public sector employees planning and working with the implementation of e-Government applications	
5	List of questions	Questions to be developed	
6	No of questions	Approximately 30	
7	Time required to develop questions	Approximately 40 hours	
8	Mode of delivery	e-Mail invitations to complete a web based questionnaire	
9	Sample size sought	200	
10	Type of sample	Purposeful – employees in the public service sector	
11	First letter	Inviting informants to contribute	

Item	Issue	Detail	Notes
12	Ethics	Questionnaire may be completed with informant name and for this a Questionnaire Informants' Information Document and a letter of consent is required. If the questionnaire is completed anonymously a letter of consent is not possible and thus not required	
13	Research Participants' Information Document	Research Participants' Information Document to accompany all invitations to participate in the research.	
14	Consent	Letter of informed consent	
15	Final letter	Thanking informants for their contribution	
16	Possible statistics	Has a statistician been consulted about how the numeric data could be analysed?	
17	Software	Have possible software packages been identified?	
18	Digital data	How will it be stored and how will it be backed up.	

Exhibit 3.2: Letter/email of invitation to complete a questionnaire

Dear Mr So-and-So

I would like to invite you to complete a questionnaire that I have constructed as part of my research on the subject of XXXXXXXX. I am inviting you as I understand that you are an authority on this topic and your opinions on this subject would be highly appreciated. No preparation work is required and the questionnaire will take between 15 and 20 minutes to complete.

I am a researcher at the Business School registered for a XXXX degree. The title of my research is XXXXXX and my principle research question is XXXXXXXXXXXXX. My research is part of the general research activity of the School and I am attaching a brochure [or including a URL] which will give you more information about the School.

I will telephone you next week to see if I can supply any further information about this request.

I will be most grateful for your help with my research.

Yours sincerely,

Researcher

Date

Exhibit 3.3: Questionnaire Informants' Information Document

The purpose of this document is to explain to potential questionnaire informants the nature of the research which is proposed and the role which he or she is being invited to play in that research.

	Issue	*Example Detail*
1	***Name of Researcher*** ***Contact Details*** ***If part-time state employers name and address***	Caroline Blue e-mail address and telephone numbers The GGG Consulting firm.
2	***Title of Research Project***	***How can the investment employed in developing and operating e-Government applications be assessed for its effectiveness?***
3	***Purpose of the Study***	The purpose of this research is to understand how e-Government investment is assessed.
4	***Description of the Study***	Academic research for a degree and/or published paper which requires primary data from individuals involved in e-Government. Specifically the role of individuals in the implementation of a range of e-Government applications.
5	***Duration of the Study***	24 months
6	***What will be your involvement and how long will it take?***	Contributors will be asked to complete a short questionnaire. The time required is estimated to be approximately 20 minutes.
7	***Why you have been asked to participate?***	You have been asked to partake in this study due to your experience with e-Government investment
8	***What will happen to the information which will be given for the study?***	The information will be held in a confidential manner while the questionnaires are being processed. Following the successful completion of the research the questionnaires will be shredded and/or destroyed.
9	***What will be done with the Results of the Study?***	The results of the questionnaire will be reported in the findings section of the research. This will be done in a completely anonymous manner.

	Issue	Example Detail
10	***What are the possible disadvantages?***	There are no costs to you associated with your involvement with this study. It is not envisaged that any negative consequences will accrue to you from your contributions in this research.
11	***In what way will the study be beneficial and to whom?***	It is hoped that this study will provide a useful framework to evaluate e-Government investment.
12	***Who has reviewed this Study to ensure that it complies with all the requirements and ethical standards of the university?***	The Ethics Committee of the School of Big Black Boxes at the Unitary College in St Lucia has approved this research proposal and granted permission for the research to commence.
13	***Can permission be withdrawn having previously been granted?***	Yes, all contributors shall retain the right to have their contributions to the research withdrawn at any time.
14	***Can you refuse to answer any question?***	Yes. The contributor has the right to refuse to answer any question on the questionnaire.

Exhibit 3.4: Letter of Informed Consent

Dear Researcher

I, Jane Doe, agree voluntarily to take part in the research project being conducted by John Brown as part of the requirements for his Doctorate/Masters Degree or Research paper at UCD. I have read the Research Participants' Information Document and I understand the contents thereof. Any questions which I have asked have been answered to my satisfaction.

I understand that the information which I will supply is confidential and that it will be anonymised and will only be used in the findings of the research.

I understand that I do not have to answer all the questions which may be put to me. The information which I provide will be held securely until the research has been completed (published) after which it will be destroyed.

The information which I provide will not be used for any other purpose.

I understand that I am entitled to ask for a de-briefing session or a copy of the research at the end of the project.

I have been informed that I may withdraw from this study at any time and that any information which I have supplied will not be used for this research and any records held relating to my contribution will be destroyed.

Signed ....

Date ....

Exhibit 3.5: A letter/email of thanks

University Name

University Address

Date

Questionnaire Informant Name

Address

Date

Dear Mr/Ms Bloggs

Thank you for having completed the questionnaire. Your input into this has been very helpful.

If you wish I would be pleased to send you an electronic copy of my dissertation or perhaps the section of my work where my findings are listed. Please let me know what you would prefer.

Yours sincerely,

Researcher

References

Brace I, 2004, Questionnaire Design, Kogan Page, London

Berdie D, J Anderson, M Niebuhr, 1986, Questionnaires: Design and Use, 2nd Ed, The Scarecrow Press, London

Bulmer M, 2004, Questionnaire, Vol. 1, Sage, Thousand Island, Ca

Gillham B, 2007, Developing a Questionnaire, 2nd , Continuum International Group, London

Goodman M, 1987, The Delphi technique: a critique, Vol 12, Issue 6, p 729-734, Journal of Advanced Nursing

Hughes J.A. (1990), The Philosophy of Science, Longmans, London.

Parasuraman A, V Zeithaml, L Berry, (1988), SERVQUAL: a multiple item scale for measuring consumer perceptions of service quality, Vol 64, Issue 1, P 12-40, Journal of Retailing

Useful websites

http://www.icbl.hw.ac.uk/ltdi/cookbook/info_questionnaires/index.html

http://www.evalued.bcu.ac.uk/tutorial/4a.htm

http://www.youtube.com/watch?v=oWPTg_VWffg

http://www.youtube.com/watch?v=31yalQIVvRY

http://www.youtube.com/watch?v=EAufRE1DMKE&feature=related

http://www.icbl.hw.ac.uk/ltdi/cookbook/info_questionnaires/index.htm l

http://www.youtube.com/watch?v=Pk1EY-_Ap_0&feature=related

http://www.youtube.com/watch?v=P9rhi7lcTls

http://www.youtube.com/watch?v=Yr_6aliPAb4

http://www.youtube.com/watch?v=GQfvocbRV3E&feature=related

http://www.lboro.ac.uk/library/skills/Advice/Questionnaire%20design.pdf

http://www.dataunitwales.gov.uk/Documents/Publications/adviceandguidance/CPS15010_Questionnaire_Design_FINAL_eng.pdf

Chapter Four
Responsibility for data concerning people

"Relativity applies to physics, not ethics"

A Einstein

4.1 Keeping of data

Anyone who holds personal data about other individuals or about the opinions of other individuals owes the individuals concerned a duty of care. Personal data may assist the aims of criminals in a number of ways, including but not limited to identity theft. Unscrupulous people could use the opinions of others to gain advantage in a number of ways, especially in a corporate setting. There are many examples of this occurring daily with the level of fraud said to be soaring. Of course, it is never possible to know how much fraud or other criminal activity related to personal details takes place, as only those activities which are discovered can be reported, and it is often said that only a small proportion of the crimes discovered are reported.

Personal data including opinions are sometimes offered more freely to academic researchers than they would be to many other types of researchers. Many members of the public see universities as important, impartial and responsible institutions.

In order to attempt to protect society against these crimes researchers need to be especially cautious about what data is acquired, how it is acquired, how it is stored and when it is to be deleted.

Universities and business schools have become concerned about the issue of data responsibility and it is for this reason, among others, that Research Ethics Committees (REC) have been established and Ethics Protocols are required. Universities are concerned about this, not only because they want to promote research of the highest ethical standard, but also because they are aware that if data acquired by academic researchers falls into the wrong hands it will or could have a major adverse effect on the reputation of the university.

4.2 Data responsibility in academic research

There are many ethical matters related to the conducting of academic research and the application for the approval of an Ethics Protocol. With regards data responsibility, which is only a relatively small part of this, there are four major matters to consider and these are:-

- The data collected from individuals who have given their informed consent should be used *only* for the purpose/s agreed upon;
- The data will be anonymised as far as is practicable as soon as possible;
- The data will need to be stored in a secure environment so that it will not fall into the hands of others by accident, mistake or by theft;
- The data will only be held as long as it is essential for the purposes of the research, after which it will be deleted in such a way that others will not be able to reconstruct or reconstitute it.

Data responsibility is only one part of the greater issue of the management and control of data in research. Many of the policies which have now been introduced by universities and business schools have been based on data protection legislation, which in the UK is legislated in terms of the Data Protection Act 1998.

The following is a brief description of the background to the Data Protection Act (DPA), the principles on which it is based, and some of the issues which arise from its acceptance as the philosophical underpinning of some of universities' rules concerning the ethics of research.

4.3 Introduction to data protection legislation

Data protection legislation is important because a number of the provisions of this legislation have been incorporated directly into university requirements for the approval of Ethics Protocols. Thus, being familiar with the DPA will assist the researcher in understanding the attitude of the Research Ethics Committee (REC) to various issues. In addition some universities are including in their Ethics Protocol application form a statement such as *"I confirm that I am aware of the provisions of the Data Protection Act (1998) and agree to comply therewith".* The DPA is substantial and the information provided here is intended to help researchers orient themselves towards the issues and will not substitute for a thorough understanding of the legislation.

By the early 1980s it was obvious that computers were beginning to play an increasingly influential role in civil society. Computer capacity had become bigger than anyone had ever dreamed. Their speed of operation (as well as their technical development) was thought to be breath-taking. Their price-power ratio was declining and unusual boxes, called microcomputers, were beginning to appear on peoples' desks and in their homes. When IBM launched its PC in 1981 the wave of personal computer ownership could be seen as unstoppable.

The Thatcher Government in the United Kingdom decided that it had better support this inevitable development and they announced the United Kingdom Information Technology Year 1982, referred to as IT82. Large numbers of organisations gave their support to the promotion of the new technology, as may be seen by the announcement of the English Spelling Society as follows:-

> *As this issue goes to press, the United Kingdom is well into its promotion and publicity for Information Technology Year 1982 when the British Government is spending £1.2 million*

to publicise modern developments in electronic communication, microprocessors, and video equipment.

All these were non-existent in their present forms only a few decades ago [sic]. Two hundred years ago, the only major piece of Information Technology was the printed word [sic]. The basis for storing information was invented several thousand years ago - the writing system.

In 1982 there will be still more marvellous developments in modern communications. Not one modern marvel will remain unchanged, unimproved. What will be the modern developments in the writing system? How much and in what way will they be influenced by computers, electronic typewriters, and typesetters, etc.? All these are already here. They will be used to the fullest extent of their capabilities!

In the Proceedings of the Third International Conference on Spelling, Research and Reform, held in Edinburgh in July, 1981 and sponsored by the Simplified Spelling Society, the possibilities for development related to IT are made more clear and convincing.

In retrospect this looks rather naive but for its time it was forward thinking in that the English Spelling Society envisaged that it would be necessary to cope with major developments in aspects of society related to data processing.

As well as the excitement about new hardware and software there was a growing realisation that there was a potential for really large increases in data and questions began to be asked concerning whether there was a need to control certain aspects of this data. The data which was of concern to those asking these questions was personal data about individual members of society.

It had been long established that the protection of privacy is a right of the individual and the collection of data, especially the large volume of data which was becoming possible with the development of Information Technology, was a concern. As a result the Data Protection Act (DPA) was introduced in the UK in 1984 and became law in

1985. The UK was not the first country to do this as Sweden had a Data Act from 1973. In 1998 a new Act was introduced in the UK as a result of an EU Data Protection Directive and the old 1984 Act was repealed.

Today many countries have enacted laws which regulate how data concerning people can be stored, processed, transferred and used. Although these laws differ from country to country there are common principles for the management of the data about which researchers should be aware. The application form for some Ethics Protocols requires the researcher to certify that he or she is familiar with the provisions of the relevant legislation and that the proposed work will comply with its provisions.

The DPA is a substantial piece of legislation and it has a reputation of being complex. Therefore from the point of view of an academic researcher it is best understood by reference to the principles which underpin it.

In addition there is the UK Freedom of Information Act (2000) which may have some impact on data held by researchers. However its impact is likely to be less than is the case with the DPA. The Freedom of Information Act (2000) supports openness and accountability, and allows individuals to call for documents, e-mails and notes held by individual staff members. If a request for information is refused then the applicant can initiate a complaints procedure. This has impacted what academics are prepared to write in e-mails and other correspondence.

4.4 DPA Principles

The four data areas of responsibility in academic research discussed above may be seen as a subset of the regulations contained in the UK DPA which regulates the use of personal data. This Act is complex and is best understood by reference to a number of principles on which it is based and these are:-

- Data may only be used for the purpose for which it was collected;

- Data may not be disclosed to other parties who are not involved with the original purpose for which the data was collected;
- Data should be held only for the time required to use it for its stated purpose;
- Adequate security measures should be in place for the storage of the data;
- Data may not be transferred outside the boundaries of the European Economic Area (EEA) unless the data is going to a country which has appropriate data protection legislation[50];
- Organisations which process data such as this need to be registered with the Information Commissioner's Office (ICO);
- People whose data is being held have a right of access to the data;
- If there is factually incorrect data then the people about whom the data is being held have the right to have the data corrected.

The regulations of this Act only apply to data which refers to living and identifiable individuals.

Anonymised or aggregated data is not regulated under this Act. Therefore statistics based on de-identified data do not fall within the purview of the Act.

For the Act to apply, data has to be held on a computer or in a relevant filing system. The notion of relevant filing systems allows/means that paper files may also fall under the purview of the Act.

4.5 The Information Commissioner's Office (ICO)

The ICO has been established to administer the provisions of the Act as well as to provide advice to organisations and individuals concerning the appropriateness of different types of activities or inter-

---

[50] The EEA includes the countries in the EU as well as Iceland, Liechtenstein and Norway.

ventions. Organisations handling personal data are required to register with the ICO and normally the university will have been registered.

The ICO works to uphold information rights in the public interest, promotes openness by public bodies and data privacy for individuals. In so doing, it has powers to make judgements as to whether the DPA is being breached and may issue Decision Notices to the offenders. In cases where there are persistent breaches the ICO can issue fines. In addition where criminal activities have occurred the ICO can initiate full legal proceedings.

In the UK the ICO has a comprehensive website at
http://www.ico.gov.uk/

4.6 Data crossing boundaries

As multinational research is on the increase, the issue of data crossing boundaries is becoming more important. Besides the European Economic Area (EEA) countries, the Data Protection Commissioners have nominated Argentina, Canada, Guernsey, Jersey, The Isle of Man and Switzerland as countries which have adequate data protection laws in place to allow data transfer from the UK. Data transfer is allowed by the Data Commissioners to other countries provided that adequate contractual arrangements can be made.

There is one other issue which relates to the cross border requirements of the DPA and it is the use of services or products such as the Internet-based Survey Monkey. This online questionnaire development service or product (and others like it) retains and stores the data obtained from a questionnaire, without stating where the data is being processed and held. Whether Survey Monkey or other such products comply with the requirements of the DPA would be unknown to the researcher and information concerning this would be difficult to ascertain, therefore the researcher should beware.

Another software product which is becoming popular with researchers is Dropbox. Once again data is uploaded and it is not clear where the data then resides and if it has crossed borders.

Individuals and organisations which use cloud computing typically do not know where their data is located. Even the providers of the cloud services may not be sure where the data is at any given moment as the computers themselves operate using optimisation algorithms which involve moving processing activates and data storage to locations which have relatively unused processing power available.

4.7 Implications for the researcher

The DPA principles impose restrictions on what the researcher can do with the data and how the researcher needs to deal with the informants who have supplied the data in the first place. It is clear that these principles have influenced how universities think about research ethics.

4.7.1 Data may only be used for the purpose for which it was collected

Research degree candidates need to explain at the outset why the data is required, which is of course to assist in the answering of the research question. Most researchers will immediately rush to declare that the data is only required for the purposes of a dissertation. This can be limiting if after the dissertation is complete the researcher wishes to use the data in pursuance of further research leading to publications in peer reviewed journals. If this is a possible requirement then it needs to be addressed in the Letter of Informed Consent at the outset. Researchers are advised to seek permission to use the data for complementary academic purposes wherever there is a possibility of so doing.

4.7.2 Data may not be disclosed to other parties who are not involved with the original purpose for which the data was collected

Although the data collected could possibly be of use for other purposes besides the research objective specified in the Ethics Protocol, this is not allowed by the DPA or by the university. The scope of the work for which the data is collected may not be allowed to creep.

4.7.3 Data should be held only for the time required to use it for its stated purpose

Academics have been traditionally unclear about how long data should be held after the research is completed. Some academics have argued that data should be available for some time in case someone wanted to replicate the study. In terms of the DPA the data should be destroyed when the dissertation is accepted and the subsequent papers are published.

4.7.4 Adequate security measures should be in place for the storage of the data

Data should always be seen as an asset and should be treated with due care and attention. Data security implies storage in a system with appropriate identification codes and passwords and that the computer on which the data is placed is not vulnerable to theft. Over the years there have been numerous incidents where laptop computers have been stolen from students and therefore researchers need to be especially cautious in this respect. When travelling the opportunity for computer loss or theft becomes even greater.

Data may not be transferred outside the boundaries of the EEA unless the data is going to a country which has appropriate data protection legislation or where an exemption has been given. If a researcher intends to use a form of cloud computing, then as a matter of course he or she should inform the informant that their data may be sent across a national boundary.

This principle was established before the arrival of cloud computing. If a cloud-based computing system is in use there is no way of knowing where the data is being stored and whether it has traversed the boundaries of the EEA.

One other point regarding boundaries. Researchers may need to send their data back to respondents, or to translators/supervisors etc. If this is done by e-mail the data is not secure. Some universities insist on the use of data encryptions. To comply with the security requirements of the DPA, researchers should use encryption services. Such services are now available from a number of suppliers.

Unfortunately it is not always possible to know to what extent these data transfer services cross boundaries. There is a paradox which is that by complying with the security aspect of the DPA you may infringe boundary requirements.

4.7.5 People whose data is being held have a right of access to the data

In the academic research environment a request from an informant to review the data he or she has supplied is unusual. However if the informant has been presented with a transcript of an interview, for example, and wishes to have some aspect of it changed, the researcher is obliged to comply with this request. This is good research practice. Similarly if errors are found then the researcher is obliged to change them.

After such a request the informant might ask to be shown the transcript again. In terms of this legislation he or she has the right to see it. Of course even without the support of the law it would be unwise to refuse to show the amended transcript to the informant, as he or she has the right to withdraw from the research at any time and have his or her data completely removed from the research.

4.7.6 If there is factually incorrect data then the people about whom the data is being held have the right to have the data corrected.

This point has been incorporated into the above as these two points are highly coupled.

4.8 Anonymising data

Mostly, the instructions supplied with the application for the approval of an Ethics Protocol state that the researcher should certify that he or she is familiar with the University's research ethics guidelines and with the data protection legislation. It is for this reason that this chapter has been written. A close inspection of the DPA and a reflection of the way that data is handled by researchers will point out that if the data is anonymised, as it will often be, the terms of the DPA do not apply.

Anonymising the data can sometimes be as simple as removing the name of an informant from a questionnaire or having entered the data from the questionnaire and after checking it, destroying the paper copy. But with regards to qualitative data, such as interviews, focus groups, video and audio recordings this can be more difficult as the informant could be recognised from his or her knowledge or opinions expressed in the interview, voice or picture. This is especially true in certain types of academic research where the description of the organisation and the function of the individual's role could lead to the identification of a particular person.

The DPA requires data not to be held for a period longer than for which it is required. This may be interpreted in different ways. For an academic degree it could be argued that when the dissertation is successfully submitted for examination the data should be deleted. On the other hand academics have usually taken the view that data should he held for a period of time in case any queries arise concerning the research. If the data has been anonymised then there should be no problem in retaining the data.

In general it is not a burdensome matter to comply with the requirements of data protection legislation and it is important to so do from both the point of view of the research and the university. There have recently been a number of unfortunate incidents reported in the press about data being lost or stolen and this has been embarrassing to the organisations concerned. Universities are anxious to avoid such publicity.

For most purposes normal courtesy and common sense will require the researcher to approach the research in such a way that the DPA will not have a great impact on the way that research is conducted in business and management studies.

4.9 Security

The issue of security is an interesting one. In terms of the researcher's handling of the data, security would cover issues such as ensuring that interview transcripts or focus group transcripts are not left lying around on the desk of the researcher in a general office. Good security practice would also suggest that the data should be copied onto a memory stick and that this storage device is lock up over night. These are simple and obvious routine issues. However, as the use of the cloud is increasing, if the data is being processed and stored on the cloud the researcher cannot have the same level of confidence that his or her data is actually secure. Questions need to be asked of the suppliers of cloud computer services before data should be submitted to them.

Keeping copies of data for back up purposes introduces another issue which is that of version control. It can be difficult to know which is the latest version of a file. To be confident in this respect requires careful naming and logging of files. This type of work is referred to by computer specialists as housekeeping and it is important. It is good practice to delete old files which we no longer require and it is important to realise that deleting a files does not remove the data from the storage device. Deleting makes it difficult to access the data but a computer specialist may be able to recover a deleted file. There are special software routines which can permanently erase the data from a computer or other storage device.

4.10 Summary

When web based research products are used it has become more difficult to know where the research data is actually located and when it will be deleted. There are concerns that some on-line facilities do not delete any data uploaded to them, although it is difficult to imagine that they will be able to hold such data in perpetuity. These have become important if not critical issues in academic research which are of material concern to university ethics committees.

The responsibility for personal data should not be seen as just another bureaucratic annoyance. It is an important aspect of academic research and the likelihood is that it will be of increasing importance in forthcoming years. It is not difficult to comply with the regulations, and in so doing the researcher obtains some protection from any possible recriminations with informants or examiners if for any reason there are problems with these groups during a latter part of the research or during examination.

References

http://www.ico.gov.uk/for_organisations/data_protection.aspx

http://dataprotectionact.org/1.html

http://www.legislation.gov.uk/ukpga/1998/29/contents

Chapter Five
Data Management – Makes writing up easier

5.1 Introduction

Although seldom if ever offered as advice, one of the first activities an academic researcher should undertake is the acquisition of a substantial filing cabinet. And due to the fact that ethics committees today require assurances that all data obtained by the researcher will be held securely, it is important that the filing cabinet has a lock and key.

With few exceptions academic research projects accumulate substantial amounts of data. The data will mainly be in the form of field notes, transcripts of interviews and focus groups, completed questionnaires, published reports, press clippings, as well as photographs, video and audio recordings.

Creating a filing system whereby the data collected by the researcher can be easily retrieved is fundamental to sound research practice. This involves the acquisition of a number of physical files in which papers collected by the researcher can be systematically stored. Some of this data may well be eventually digitised and stored on a computer, but there will always be the need to secure the original source documents. These original source documents are the ultimate backup for the researcher and they should be kept for some time, even after the end of the research.

There are numerous different types of filing systems and each researcher will need to choose what will suit him or her best. Some of these filing systems can be expensive while others are simple, inexpensive and easy to use.

5.2 Data Management and Data Integrity

Some academics suggest that data integrity should be considered under the heading of data management. Others suggest that it is a subject in its own right. The issue of data integrity addresses how the researcher ensures that the data collected is correct, complete and that no errors creep into the data when it is recorded or transfer from one medium to another. Some researchers argue that data is the most precious asset which the researcher acquires and that he or she needs to be aware of the problems which can arise and to be continually vigilant that correct, relevant, up-to-date and not corrupted data is being used in the research.

It is always the responsibility of the researcher to ensure the integrity of the data.

5.3 Some details of which you should be aware

Much of what can be said about data management for academics will be regarded by many researchers to be common sense. However it is a well known fact that common sense is not all that common and thus it is worthwhile taking a few pages to point out some of the issues and making a few suggestions. Effective data management planning can prevent a number of problems occurring and facilitate an early completion of the research.

Data management may be defined in this context as putting in place procedures and practices which will prevent data loss from delaying or disrupting a research project. Of course it is not sufficient to define or simply specify these procedures and practices. They have to be conscientiously followed and this is quite difficult for many researchers. Despite the tedium involved, taking care of your work is of prime importance. Even if you back up regularly to an offsite location, data loss of data the one time that you forget to do this can cause you a lot of grief – especially if it happens when you are close to submission and under pressure from deadlines.

In the production of a research dissertation a large amount of writing is necessary. In addition there will often be numerous graphs and diagrams as well as other figures and tables generated by software packages. Preparation of a dissertation will normally involve a word processor, a spreadsheet and possibly other presentation software not to mention statistical packages such as SPSS or analysis tools such as nVivo. Some doctorates may have sufficient data to justify using a relational or other structured database. Microsoft has by far the leading position in the market for office software and thus the most likely systems will be Word, Excel and PowerPoint. It is beyond the scope of this book to address specific issues related to these products but nonetheless it may be helpful to consider some of the data or file management issues associated with a large research project when using these tools.

5.4 Directory and file names

How documents are filed in the computer can make the researcher's work relatively easy or it can lead to confusion and the need for rework. Without proper file management documents can be lost or can be inappropriately deleted. Any reworking is wasteful and should wherever possible be avoided. The first issue here is that an easy-to-use directory and file naming system is required. The second issue is that it is essential to create and maintain a backup regime throughout the research project. Devising the correct structure on day one can save you many hours of work later, so this deserves a bit of thought before you set it up.

5.5 Directories and subdirectories

The first step is to create and name a master directory for all the files related to the research project on the disk of your principal computer. Within this directory there will be the need for a number of subdirectories. The number and the content of these subdirectories will depend to a considerable extent on the type of research being undertaken. It will also depend on the data management style of the researcher. Planning the layout of these directories can be helpful to the smooth operation and this plan could be seen as a road map to the data required for the dissertation write-up.

If empirical research is being conducted it may be useful to have a subdirectory for the data collected and a separate subdirectory for the writing up. If different types of data are involved a researcher might choose to have one subdirectory for quantitative data which might be in Excel files and another subdirectory for qualitative data, which could be in Word files. Depending upon the software used to analyse the data, more files of different types will be created and it may be appropriate to store these in different directories. As a general rule do not nest directories more than two or three times as deeply nested directories can cause data to be forgotten or mislaid.

Within the writing up subdirectory some researchers like to create another level of subdirectories, one for each chapter in the dissertation and one each for the appendices and the references (if the latter are not stored in something like EndNote). This can be useful as there will no doubt be a number of different versions of the text for each chapter and a large number of files can be confusing. It is important to incorporate a version indicator usually a number or date in the file title. It is hard to over-emphasise the importance of version control. Losing track of which version is current can be frustrating and can waste a lot of valuable time. In a worst case scenario it can lead to errors in the dissertation.

On the question of version control another problem which may arise is having to deal with many old versions of the same file. Good practice with computer housekeeping requires old versions of files to be deleted when new versions are in use and have been backed up correctly.

There is an art in file and directory naming. Try to design something simple, meaningful and flexible. Do not set up too many directories; keep it manageable.

5.6 Merging files or combining data

As the write-up develops there may be the need to merge files with text and files with data such as tables, diagrams or graphs. On this account it is important to be aware of the size of the resulting file.

The file size can grow surprisingly large and not all computers (or e-mail systems) operate well with large files although this is a diminishing problem. There are techniques for controlling the size of files and researchers should become familiar with these. Particular attention should be given to image files as the file type and resolution will affect both the appearance and the size of the resulting file. Furthermore, if images are copied into a text file and then cropped, it is a good idea to then cut them from the text file and paste them back into the document so as to lose the cropped data from the file.

As the file size grows the researcher should take more care with regular saving and backing up procedures as there is obviously more to lose.

5.7 Backing up data

Many researchers will lose some data at some time during the research project. The loss of data is painful and may actually put the whole research project in jeopardy. Researchers who do not make adequate arrangements for backing up are effectively gambling with this project.

As a general rule you should back up every day during periods of moderate activity and several times a day during periods of intense writing and/or analysis. Many universities provide an automated backup service and you can use this if it is available, but during highly active periods it may not be frequent enough. If not, you should have your own backup to a reliable medium which is kept offsite in a safe location. The minimum number of backups is one, but two is advisable. This is often referred to as a 'father and grandfather' system whereby you overwrite the day before yesterday's backup with today's backup. Where files are not too big, a simple and effective form of backup is to e-mail the files to a friend and ask them to keep the copy in their mail system. You can also mail the backups to yourself though if your file sizes are large, you will need to pay attention to your assigned mailbox space.

Be careful in your choice of backup media. Traditionally most researchers use a secondary storage unit directly under their control with which to back up their data. Until relatively recently this might have been a CD or a DVD or some sort of fast tape machine. Increasingly, memory sticks also known as flash or pen drives are now being used for this purpose. Although excellent in many respects these memory sticks are vulnerable especially to loss, theft (and failure). To overcome this, researchers sometimes keep a number of copies of their data and write-up and this can in turn lead to version identification problems (see below). If you have a particularly large volume of data it may be worth buying a small portable hard disk drive. These are inexpensive and more robust than the flash drive technology.

Another approach to backing up is to use cloud based services supplied by a number of major companies globally. If you do this, the backing up process can be looked after by the outsourcer and your data will be stored in various parts of the world. On the face of it this arrangement appears to offer many advantages and can offer peace of mind to the researcher. However many countries have data protection legislation and this can proscribe that certain types of data cannot be transmitted across national borders of certain countries. Bear in mind too that while some cloud providers offer quite low cost options for moderate amounts of data storage, costs can rise steeply if you go over a certain threshold. It is not likely that many dissertations will do this, but check the fine print before signing any agreement with a cloud supplier.

Whatever approach is taken to backing up it is important to test its effectiveness from time to time. Computers are not infallible and data can be corrupted. The researcher should be reasonably confident that the data can be restored in a useful way.

Finally as regards backing up, because computer technology now plays such an important role in research it is often forgotten that taking a paper copy of data and partial write-ups is also a backup – perhaps the backup of the last resort.

5.8 Reference management software

Another strand of data which needs planning and control is the recording of detailed references used in the dissertation. Irrespective of whether or not empirical research is being undertaken, the researcher will be required to demonstrate that a large number of the published works of others has been read and understood. This reading needs to be recorded in a reference list and there are today a number of specialised products which can assist with this task. EndNote is one of the best known. However the reference list may also be created in a word processor such as Word or another database type product.

5.9 Summary and conclusion

Like so many other issues in research, with a little data management and contingency planning many tedious problems can be avoided.

The first step is to create a road map of how the different types of files will be stored on a directory by directory basis.

The second step is to create a standard for file naming with a strong emphasis on the fact that many files will have multiple versions.

The third step is to be aware of the implications of large files.

The last step is to decide your backup policy and ensure that these backup arrangements are satisfactory and in particular that they will work if and when they are needed.

Appendices

Appendix 1: Qualitative Questionnaire

The IT Management Research Series
Active Benefit Realisation
Questionnaire

This questionnaire may be completed either anonymously or the informant may supply his or her work details. If the questionnaire is completed anonymously then by returning the questionnaire to me the informant is consenting to my using the data therein for my research and I am being granted permission to have the results published. The data will be used only for academic purposes and all the provisions of the Data Protection Act will be complied with.

If the informant wishes to disclose his or her work details then he or she is required to complete the Letter of Informed Consent which is attached.

This questionnaire is part of a research study into how information systems development may be managed in order to maximise the potential benefits which can be derived from the use of the technology. The questionnaire is concerned with substantial information systems projects which affect a number of users. Thus, it is concerned with departmental information systems, or enterprise wide information systems. However, the research is independent of any consideration of either hardware or software platforms in use.

The questionnaire should not take more than 30 minutes to complete. All information supplied by respondents will be treated with the utmost confidence and sources of the information will not be disclosed. Thank you very much for your assistance in this research.

Professor Dan Remenyi
Department of IS
Faculty of Commerce

Part 1 - The business opportunity or problem identification and validation

1. Does your organisation have a formal procedure for identifying business opportunities or problems?

   Yes ☐ No ☐

2. If the answer to question 1 is yes, briefly describe how this formal procedure operates.

   ___

3. If the answer to question 1 is no, how are business opportunities or problems identified?

   ___

4. How frequently does IT play a role in assisting your organisation to exploit a business opportunity or to solve a business problem?

   All the time ☐
   Some of the time ☐
   Occasionally ☐
   Hardly ever ☐

5. If IT is hardly ever perceived as a facilitating agent to assist your organisation with its business opportunities or problems, what do you regard as the main purpose or function of your information technology?

   ___

6. When IT is identified as an important aspect of the solution to the business problem or opportunity, who normally points out the role which IT can play?

   IT staff ☐
   Eventual users of the system ☐
   Administrators ☐
   Consultants ☐
   Others (Please specify) ___

7. Does your answer to question 6 differ depending on the size of the project or the type of application?

   Yes ☐ No ☐

8. If the size of the project is critical is that size measured in terms of person years, money amounts or other?

____

9. Is a formal definition of a business problem or opportunity produced?

 Yes ☐ No ☐

10. If the answer to question 9 is yes, what does the formal definition look like?

 Half page written description ☐
 Calculation of cost reduction or profit improvement ☐
 Other (please specify)___________________________

11. Proposed or suggested IT projects may sometimes be inappropriate, i.e. too expensive or inconsistent with the organisation strategy. How do you check to see if the proposed IT system is relevant and appropriate?

____

12. In performing a relevance and appropriateness check which of the following do you use?

 Strategic alignment test ☐
 Internal benchmarking ☐
 External benchmarking ☐
 Brainstorming techniques ☐
 Some other technique (please specify) _______________

Part 2 - Stakeholder issues

13. How many different types of stakeholders are typically involved or concerned with a major IT project?

____

14. Although each project will have a different set of stakeholders, are there certain groups of stakeholders which will be involved in almost all projects? If so who are these?

____

15. How are appropriate stakeholders identified and who does this identification?

---

16. Are formal stakeholder meetings convened?

    Yes ☐ No ☐

17. If the answer to question 16 is yes, how frequently are these meetings held?

---

18. On the assumption that there are primary and secondary stakeholders of the IT project, which stakeholders would you normally regard for a typical project as primary and which as secondary?

---

19. Are the eventual users of the systems always included among the stakeholders?

    Yes ☐ No ☐

20. If the answer to question 19 is yes, how influential is the eventual owner in the project decision making?

---

21. Do you attempt to involve top management (someone at director level or someone reporting to a director) as a stakeholder?

    Yes ☐ No ☐

22. If the answer to question 21 is yes, would you attempt to sustain the attention of top management throughout the project and if so how would you do this?

---

23. How important is the issue of partnership between the stakeholders?

    Essential ☐
    Very ☐
    Quite ☐
    Not at all ☐

24. If you consider the issue of partnership to be essential or very important how do you attempt to create a partnership approach and how successful are you in this endeavour?

____

25. Who makes the final decision whether to proceed with an IT project?

    Senior managers ☐
    Eventual users ☐
    IT staff ☐
    Accountants and administrators ☐
    Others, (please specify) ________________________

26. At what stage in the project is the eventual ownership of an information systems project identified?

    At the outset ☐
    When the project is authorised ☐
    During project production ☐
    At testing ☐
    When the project is commissioned ☐

27. How are the eventual owners of the information system identified?

____

Part Three - Feasibility study issues

28. Does your organisation generally perform a formal information systems feasibility study?

    Yes ☐ No ☐

29. If the answer to question 28 is yes, are information systems costs and benefits estimated?

    Yes ☐ No ☐

30. If the answer to question 29 is no, how are the decision criteria for approving an information systems project presented?

____

31. If the answer to question 29 is yes, how are these cost estimates obtained?

    Vendor supplied ☐
    From internal know-how ☐
    Use consultants ☐
    Others, (please specify) __________________________

32. When benefits are estimated, how is this done?

Stated as financial numbers in the form of single point estimates ☐
Stated as financial numbers in the form of range estimates ☐
Stated as business issues such as higher customer satisfaction ☐
Other, (please specify) __________________________

33. If benefits are stated as business issues such as higher customer satisfaction how will it be established whether these benefits have been, in due course delivered?

    ____

34. Are any benefits, either financial or business, validated as appropriate by establishing whether they are aligned with the organisation's corporate CSF?

    ____

35. If financial figures are used in the feasibility study which investment indicator is calculated?

    Payback ☐
    ROI ☐
    NPV ☐
    IRR ☐
    Other, (please specify) __________________________

36. Are solution alternatives considered as part of the process of deciding whether or not to proceed with a project?

    ____

37. At what stage, if ever, do your project management procedures address the question of risk?

    ____

38. Could risks be identified and associated with different benefits, different CSFs and different stakeholders?

___

39. Does the feasibility study or any other aspect of the preparation process for a project require an outcome statement?

___

Part Four - Culture gap issues

40. Sometimes there are language difficulties in discussing information systems, especially when information systems staff and eventual users have to exchange ideas about a system. How do you attempt to minimise communication problems between these groups?

___

41. At the time of the project being initiated which of the following issues have been resolved?

The budget	☐
Who the systems champion will be	☐
The system delivery date	☐
The test data	☐
User's responsibility	☐
Systems ownership	☐
Strategic implication of the system	☐

Other, (please specify) ___

42. How long does it typically take (in months) from systems concept initialisation to project approval?

___

Details of informant and the organisation optional. Please read carefully the paragraphs on ethics at the start of the questionnaire.

Appendix 2: The Measurement of IS Effectiveness

The following questionnaire has been designed to help assess the effectiveness of the corporate information systems used to support the firm in achieving its objectives. This user satisfaction approach to measuring the effectiveness of information systems is used extensively in businesses throughout the world.

The questionnaire has been divided into four parts.

Part A relates to demographic details about your position in the firm.

Parts B and C use the same set of 35 statements but answered from two different perspectives.

Part D contains one specific question as well as an opportunity for you to provide open-ended comment on the systems.

Your responses to the statements in Part B refer to your expectations, given an ideal situation, of your firm's information systems. Your answers to the second set of 35 questions in Part C refer to how the Information Systems Department of the firm actually performs in terms of these systems attributes. Finally, in Part D we would like you to rate your overall opinion of the information systems, and we would welcome any comments that you would like to make concerning your own experience with the Information Systems Department in respect of its effectiveness. The questionnaire uses a nine-point scale where 1 means you Strongly disagree and 9 means you Strongly agree. For each statement please tick the number that corresponds to your level of agreement. Please do not tick or circle between the numbers.

For example, if you agree quite strongly with the statement 'I expect ease of access to computer facilities' your rating in the first set of statements could be:

Strongly Disagree 1 ☐ 2☐ 3☐ 4☐ 5 ☐ 6 ☐ 7☐ 8☐✓ 9☐ Strongly agree

If you do not agree that the performance of the Information Systems Department in actually providing these facilities is particularly good, your rating in the second set of statements might be:

Strongly Disagree 1 ☐ 2☐ 3☐✓ 4☐ 5 ☐ 6 ☐ 7☐ 8☐ 9☐ Strongly agree

Please ensure that all statements are rated by ticking one and only one response.

The questionnaire should not take more than 15-20 minutes to complete. All information supplied by respondents will be treated with the utmost confidence. Your views will only be reported in summary. The data will be stored securely until the research project has been completed at which point the questionnaires will be shredded and the computer files deleted. Thank you very much for your assistance in this research. Please return your completed questionnaire to the survey administrator.

Professor Dan Remenyi
IT Effectiveness Assessment Services

PART A

Please supply the following information about your position:

1. In which department or section do you work (Tick one)?

Inland Operations ___
Coastal Operations ___
Operations Services ___
Water Resource Management ___
Infrastructure Planning ___
Strategic planning ___
Public Affairs ___
Information Services ___
New Works ___
Water Quality ___
Analytical Services ___
Process Services ___
unused ___
Geographic Information Systems ___
unused ___
Finance & Administration ___
Human Resources ___
Other, Please Specify ___________________________

2. How many years have you been working in the organisation?

____

3. How many years experience have you had working with a PC or terminal?

____

4. How many years experience have you had working with a PC network or mainframe?

____

5. How many hours per week do you use a PC or a PC network or mainframe?

____

PART B - Expectations under ideal circumstances

Please respond by ticking the number that corresponds to how much you agree or disagree with the following statements of expectation, given an ideal situation.

		Strongly Disagree ... Strongly Agree
1.	I expect ease of access to computing facilities.	1__ 2__ 3__ 4__ 5__ 6__ 7__ 8__ 9__
2.	I expect up-to-date hardware.	1__ 2__ 3__ 4__ 5__ 6__ 7__ 8__ 9__
3.	I expect up-to-date software.	1__ 2__ 3__ 4__ 5__ 6__ 7__ 8__ 9__
4.	I expect access to external databases.	1__ 2__ 3__ 4__ 5__ 6__ 7__ 8__ 9__
5.	I expect a low percentage of hardware and software downtime.	1__ 2__ 3__ 4__ 5__ 6__ 7__ 8__ 9__

		Strongly Disagree / Strongly Agree
6.	I expect a high degree of technical competence from systems support staff.	1__ 2__ 3__ 4__ 5__ 6__ 7__ 8__ 9__
7.	I expect to have a high level of confidence in the systems I use.	1__ 2__ 3__ 4__ 5__ 6__ 7__ 8__ 9__
8.	I expect to have a high degree of personal control over the systems I use.	1__ 2__ 3__ 4__ 5__ 6__ 7__ 8__ 9__
9.	I expect the ISD to be responsive to my changing needs.	1__ 2__ 3__ 4__ 5__ 6__ 7__ 8__ 9__
10.	I expect confidentiality for my own data.	1__ 2__ 3__ 4__ 5__ 6__ 7__ 8__ 9__
11.	I expect a provision for disaster recovery.	1__ 2__ 3__ 4__ 5__ 6__ 7__ 8__ 9__
12.	I expect piracy avoidance procedures to be in place.	1__ 2__ 3__ 4__ 5__ 6__ 7__ 8__ 9__
13.	I expect excellent systems response time.	1__ 2__ 3__ 4__ 5__ 6__ 7__ 8__ 9__
14.	I expect excellent technical training.	1__ 2__ 3__ 4__ 5__ 6__ 7__ 8__ 9__
15.	I expect fast response time from support staff to remedy problems.	1__ 2__ 3__ 4__ 5__ 6__ 7__ 8__ 9__

		Strongly Disagree / Strongly Agree
16.	I expect to participate in the planning of system technology requirements.	1__ 2__ 3__ 4__ 5__ 6__ 7__ 8__ 9__
17.	I expect a positive attitude from support staff.	1__ 2__ 3__ 4__ 5__ 6__ 7__ 8__ 9__
18.	I expect overall cost-effectiveness from information technology.	1__ 2__ 3__ 4__ 5__ 6__ 7__ 8__ 9__
19.	I expect the use of IT to improve my personal productivity.	1__ 2__ 3__ 4__ 5__ 6__ 7__ 8__ 9__
20.	I expect the use of IT to enrich my working experience.	1__ 2__ 3__ 4__ 5__ 6__ 7__ 8__ 9__
21.	I expect standardisation of hardware.	1__ 2__ 3__ 4__ 5__ 6__ 7__ 8__ 9__
22.	I expect excellent documentation to support technical training.	1__ 2__ 3__ 4__ 5__ 6__ 7__ 8__ 9__
23.	I expect help to make the most of my application software.	1__ 2__ 3__ 4__ 5__ 6__ 7__ 8__ 9__
24.	I expect to be able to communicate by e-mail with colleagues.	1__ 2__ 3__ 4__ 5__ 6__ 7__ 8__ 9__
25.	I expect to have access to the World Wide Web	1__ 2__ 3__ 4__ 5__ 6__ 7__ 8__ 9__

		Strongly Disagree / Strongly Agree
26.	I expect to find the time to learn the systems I use.	1_ 2_ 3_ 4_ 5_ 6_ 7_ 8_ 9_
27.	I expect there to be a service level agreement in place.	1_ 2_ 3_ 4_ 5_ 6_ 7_ 8_ 9_
28.	I expect IS professionals to monitor their performance in delivering IT services to me.	1_ 2_ 3_ 4_ 5_ 6_ 7_ 8_ 9_
29.	I expect prompt processing of requests for changes to existing systems.	1_ 2_ 3_ 4_ 5_ 6_ 7_ 8_ 9_
30.	I expect IT to be aligned to the overall corporate plan.	1_ 2_ 3_ 4_ 5_ 6_ 7_ 8_ 9_
31.	I expect there to be short lead times for the development of new systems.	1_ 2_ 3_ 4_ 5_ 6_ 7_ 8_ 9_
32.	I expect systems analysts to understand my business requirements.	1_ 2_ 3_ 4_ 5_ 6_ 7_ 8_ 9_
33.	I expect a high degree of flexibility in the system with regards data and reports.	1_ 2_ 3_ 4_ 5_ 6_ 7_ 8_ 9_
34.	I expect the portfolio of software applications available to me to be continually increased.	1_ 2_ 3_ 4_ 5_ 6_ 7_ 8_ 9_

		Strongly Disagree — Strongly Agree
35.	I expect the benefits derived by myself from the systems I use to be measured.	1__ 2__ 3__ 4__ 5__ 6__ 7__ 8__ 9__

PART C – Actual Performance

Please respond by ticking the number that corresponds to how much you agree or disagree with the following statements of performance, i.e. what actually happens.

		Strongly Disagree — Strongly Agree
1.	I have easy access to computing facilities.	1__ 2__ 3__ 4__ 5__ 6__ 7__ 8__ 9__
2.	I have up-to-date hardware.	1__ 2__ 3__ 4__ 5__ 6__ 7__ 8__ 9__
3.	I have up-to-date software.	1__ 2__ 3__ 4__ 5__ 6__ 7__ 8__ 9__
4.	I have access to external databases.	1__ 2__ 3__ 4__ 5__ 6__ 7__ 8__ 9__
5.	I experience a low percentage of hardware and software downtime.	1__ 2__ 3__ 4__ 5__ 6__ 7__ 8__ 9__
6.	I experience a high degree of technical competence from systems support staff.	1__ 2__ 3__ 4__ 5__ 6__ 7__ 8__ 9__

		Strongly Disagree — Strongly Agree
7.	I experience a high level of confidence in the systems I use.	1__ 2__ 3__ 4__ 5__ 6__ 7__ 8__ 9__
8.	I have a high degree of personal control over the systems I use.	1__ 2__ 3__ 4__ 5__ 6__ 7__ 8__ 9__
9.	The ISD is responsive to my changing needs.	1__ 2__ 3__ 4__ 5__ 6__ 7__ 8__ 9__
10.	I have confidence in the confidentiality for my own data.	1__ 2__ 3__ 4__ 5__ 6__ 7__ 8__ 9__
11.	I am satisfied with the provisions made for disaster recovery.	1__ 2__ 3__ 4__ 5__ 6__ 7__ 8__ 9__
12.	I am satisfied with the provisions made for piracy avoidance.	1__ 2__ 3__ 4__ 5__ 6__ 7__ 8__ 9__
13.	I experience excellent systems response time.	1__ 2__ 3__ 4__ 5__ 6__ 7__ 8__ 9__
14.	I receive excellent technical training.	1__ 2__ 3__ 4__ 5__ 6__ 7__ 8__ 9__
15.	I experience fast response time from support staff to remedy problems.	1__ 2__ 3__ 4__ 5__ 6__ 7__ 8__ 9__
16.	I participate in the planning of system technology requirements.	1__ 2__ 3__ 4__ 5__ 6__ 7__ 8__ 9__

		Strongly Disagree — Strongly Agree
17.	I experience a positive attitude from support staff.	1__ 2__ 3__ 4__ 5__ 6__ 7__ 8__ 9__
18.	I am satisfied with the overall cost-effectiveness of our information technology.	1__ 2__ 3__ 4__ 5__ 6__ 7__ 8__ 9__
19.	The use of IT improves my personal productivity.	1__ 2__ 3__ 4__ 5__ 6__ 7__ 8__ 9__
20.	The use of IT enriches my working experience.	1__ 2__ 3__ 4__ 5__ 6__ 7__ 8__ 9__
21.	I have standardisation of hardware.	1__ 2__ 3__ 4__ 5__ 6__ 7__ 8__ 9__
22.	I receive excellent documentation to support technical training.	1__ 2__ 3__ 4__ 5__ 6__ 7__ 8__ 9__
23.	I receive help to make the most of my application software.	1__ 2__ 3__ 4__ 5__ 6__ 7__ 8__ 9__
24.	I am able to communicate by e-mail with colleagues.	1__ 2__ 3__ 4__ 5__ 6__ 7__ 8__ 9__
25.	I have access to the World Wide Web	1__ 2__ 3__ 4__ 5__ 6__ 7__ 8__ 9__
26.	I find the time to learn the systems I use.	1__ 2__ 3__ 4__ 5__ 6__ 7__ 8__ 9__
27.	There is a service level agreement in place.	1__ 2__ 3__ 4__ 5__ 6__ 7__ 8__ 9__

		Strongly Disagree — Strongly Agree
28.	IS professionals monitor their performance in delivering IT services me.	1__ 2__ 3__ 4__ 5__ 6__ 7__ 8__ 9__
29.	I experience prompt processing of requests for changes to existing systems.	1__ 2__ 3__ 4__ 5__ 6__ 7__ 8__ 9__
30.	IT is aligned to the overall corporate plan.	1__ 2__ 3__ 4__ 5__ 6__ 7__ 8__ 9__
31.	I experience short lead times for the development of new systems.	1__ 2__ 3__ 4__ 5__ 6__ 7__ 8__ 9__
32.	Systems analysts do understand my business requirements.	1__ 2__ 3__ 4__ 5__ 6__ 7__ 8__ 9__
33.	I experience a high degree of flexibility in the system with regards data and reports.	1__ 2__ 3__ 4__ 5__ 6__ 7__ 8__ 9__
34.	The portfolio of software applications available to me continually increases.	1__ 2__ 3__ 4__ 5__ 6__ 7__ 8__ 9__
35.	The benefits derived by myself from the systems I use are measured.	1__ 2__ 3__ 4__ 5__ 6__ 7__ 8__ 9__

Please rate your **overall opinion** of the quality of the IS Service offered to you.

		Strongly Disagree Strongly Agree
	On the whole IS Services perform well considering all the challenges they face.	1__ 2__ 3__ 4__ 5__ 6__ 7__ 8__ 9__

Please supply any further comments you wish concerning the effectiveness of your computer network system. Your comments will not be attributed to you but will only be used as input into the general analysis of the systems.

____

____

____

____

Many thanks for your help with this survey.

Appendix 3: Delphi Study

A Three Round Delphi Study

A study in e-Government

The Delphi technique is a group consensus making process that has been proven over a number of years to be a valuable tool in attempting to produce a consensus in the opinions from a group of experts. It was designed to assist executives in the collection and analysis of expert opinion in order to understand issues and trends.

In Delphi studies opinions are collected by the use of a questionnaire which in this case relates attributes an individual needs for a successful academic career.

In this study you are asked to state how strongly you disagree or agree with a series of 20 statements on a scale of 1 to 9 where 1 indicates that you strongly disagree and 9 indicates that you strongly agree.

In order to attempt to reach a level of consensus on each of these issues you will be asked to complete the same questions three times. On the second and third occasions you will be asked to re-evaluate your responses in the light of the average response to each question that was given by the whole group in the previous round. You will also be provided with the standard deviation of the groups scores on a question by question basis.

It is fully appreciated that there will be different opinions regarding what constitutes success but as this study will only include senior academics it is likely that there will be some general agreement on this issue.

Please give your opinion of the following issues.

Name .... Round #1

		Strongly Disagree — Strongly Agree
1.	The pressure to modernise government.	1__ 2__ 3__ 4__ 5__ 6__ 7__ 8__ 9__
2.	The need to contain government expenses and thus keep tax from increasing.	1__ 2__ 3__ 4__ 5__ 6__ 7__ 8__ 9__
3.	The short time horizon of a government i.e. 5 year	1__ 2__ 3__ 4__ 5__ 6__ 7__ 8__ 9__
4.	Lack of knowledge within government departments as to how to justify governments' investment.	1__ 2__ 3__ 4__ 5__ 6__ 7__ 8__ 9__
5.	Complicated internal bureaucratic policy requirements by governmental departments.	1__ 2__ 3__ 4__ 5__ 6__ 7__ 8__ 9__
6.	Attitude of outsourcers to government contracts.	1__ 2__ 3__ 4__ 5__ 6__ 7__ 8__ 9__
7.	Civil servants struggle to manage outsourced contract	1__ 2__ 3__ 4__ 5__ 6__ 7__ 8__ 9__
8.	Governments outsourcing processes is complicated.	1__ 2__ 3__ 4__ 5__ 6__ 7__ 8__ 9__

		Strongly Disagree — Strongly Agree
9.	Civil servants do not understand the need for outsourcing.	1__ 2__ 3__ 4__ 5__ 6__ 7__ 8__ 9__
10.	Integrating civil servants and outsourced team members is difficult.	1__ 2__ 3__ 4__ 5__ 6__ 7__ 8__ 9__
11.	The influence of politicians.	1__ 2__ 3__ 4__ 5__ 6__ 7__ 8__ 9__
12.	Interference by government Ministers.	1__ 2__ 3__ 4__ 5__ 6__ 7__ 8__ 9__
13.	Is influenced by policy shift within government.	1__ 2__ 3__ 4__ 5__ 6__ 7__ 8__ 9__
14.	Civil servants are generally not sufficiently technologically savvy to understand the consequences of their decisions on the project.	1__ 2__ 3__ 4__ 5__ 6__ 7__ 8__ 9__
15.	Civil servants decision making processes are complex and bureaucratic.	1__ 2__ 3__ 4__ 5__ 6__ 7__ 8__ 9__
16.	The scarcity of in-house ICT expertise and resources.	1__ 2__ 3__ 4__ 5__ 6__ 7__ 8__ 9__

		Strongly Disagree — Strongly Agree
17.	The tendency towards 'turf wars' within government departments.	1__ 2__ 3__ 4__ 5__ 6__ 7__ 8__ 9__
18.	Civil servants inability to understand the point of view of the citizen.	1__ 2__ 3__ 4__ 5__ 6__ 7__ 8__ 9__
19.	Is affected by challengers of competition from other governmental departments.	1__ 2__ 3__ 4__ 5__ 6__ 7__ 8__ 9__
20.	Civil servants often do not know what is actually required from the system/project.	1__ 2__ 3__ 4__ 5__ 6__ 7__ 8__ 9__

	Groupings of the questions	Grouping
1	The pressure to modernise government.	Complexity
2	The need to contain government expenses and thus keep tax from increasing.	
3	The short time horizon of a government i.e. 5 year	
4	Lack of knowledge within government departments as to how to justify governments' investment.	
5	Complicated internal bureaucratic policy requirements by governmental departments.	
6	Attitude of outsourcers to government contracts.	Outsourcing
7	Civil servants struggle to manage outsourced contract	
8	Governments outsourcing processes is complicated.	
9	Civil servants do not understand the need for outsourcing.	
10	Integrating civil servants and outsourced team members is difficult.	
11	The influence of politicians.	Leadership
12	Interference by government Ministers.	
13	Is influenced by policy shift within government.	
14	Civil servants are generally not sufficiently technologically savvy to understand the consequences of their decisions on the project.	
15	Civil servants decision making processes are complex and bureaucratic.	
16	The scarcity of in-house ICT expertise and resources.	Stakeholder
17	The tendency towards 'turf wars' within government departments.	
18	Civil servants inability to understand the point of view of the citizen.	
19	Is affected by challengers of competition from other governmental departments.	
20	Civil servants often do not know what is actually required from the system/project.	

This particular Delphi study allowed the individual questions to be grouped under four major headings which were Complexity, Outsourcing, Leadership and Stakeholders.

Results of Round 1				
Score Order	**Q'aire Order**	**Questions**	**Avg**	**STD**
1	**9**	Civil servants do not understand the need for outsourcing.	4.82	1.60
2	**19**	Is affected by challengers of competition from other governmental departments.	5.16	1.65
3	**2**	The need to contain government expenses and thus keep tax from increasing.	5.54	1.68
4	**10**	Integrating civil servants and outsourced team members is difficult.	5.58	1.75
5	**3**	Short time horizon of a government i.e. 5 year	5.67	1.80
6	**6**	Attitude of outsourcers to government contracts.	5.76	1.85
7	**18**	Civil servants inability to understand the point of view of the citizen.	5.88	1.86
8	**4**	Lack of knowledge within government departments to justify governments' investment.	5.90	1.86
9	**8**	Governments outsourcing processes is complicated.	5.94	1.87
10	**7**	Civil servants struggle to manage outsourced contract	6.00	1.89
11	**1**	The pressure to modernise government.	6.38	1.90
12	**12**	Interference by government Ministers.	6.42	1.93
13	**20**	Civil servants often do not know what is actually required from the system/project.	6.42	1.94
14	**14**	Civil servants are generally not sufficiently technologically savvy to understand the consequences of their decisions on the project.	6.54	1.94
15	**13**	Is influenced by policy shift within government.	6.64	1.96
16	**17**	The tendency towards 'turf wars' within government departments.	6.68	1.96
17	**11**	The influence of politicians.	6.78	2.11
18	**15**	Civil servants decision making processes are complex and bureaucratic.	6.86	2.13
19	**5**	Complicated internal bureaucratic policy requirements by governmental departments.	6.94	2.16
20	**16**	Scarcity of in-house ICT expertise & resources.	6.98	2.20

The above report shows the results of the round number 1 of a Delphi study this report is then dispatched to all the participants together with an additional column which provides them with an opportunity to reconsider their original score. Their changed is then used to recalculate the results of Round 2.

Round 2 results in a report similar to above, which is again dispatched to the Delphi study participants and they are then invited for the third and last time to consider their position.

Appendix 4: Interviews as 'talk tangos'

Obtaining reliable data from informants through the process of interviewing is a challenge. It is by no means obvious that the informant and the researcher will always understand each other. When a question is asked of anyone there is always the issue of how well it has been heard and understood. Then there is the question of whether the answer has been heard by the researcher correctly.

Confirming the reply given to the question is a recognised way of establishing the level of understanding between the two individuals. One of the approaches to confirming this understanding is for the researcher to summarise the reply in his or her own words and to ask the informant for confirmation that what is now being said is a correct reflection or interpretation of what the informant has intended. It is for this reason that some researchers tend to think about a research interview as actually being a conversation, albeit a highly controlled conversation. To signal the conversational nature of an interview, this event is sometimes described as an *inter view* where the usual form of the word is split into two.

Reflecting on the issue of how conversations operate the metaphor of the 'talk tango' is useful. In his book, Once Upon A Number, Paulos (1998)[51] expands upon the issue of the challenge of understanding one another. Paulos uses the term 'talk tango' to describe how people in conversation grow to understand each other on a progressive basis. This term represents a particularly interesting metaphor as it is easy to imagine the different moves and positions that dancers go through when they perform a tango and conversations which lead to understanding can often be no less involved and challenging. One of the main messages which is contained in the metaphor of the 'talk tango' is that understanding is not instant and that the researcher and the informant have to strive deliberately at be-

[51] Paulos J, 1998, Once Upon A Number, p14, The Penguin Press, London

ing understood, in a similar way to tango dancers who have to focus intensely on their coordination.

In academic research the onus is on the researcher to ensure that he or she is confident that the replies offered by the informant represent the informant's considered answer to the question that has been put to him or to her. This responsibility should not be taken lightly as the integrity of the research is directly dependent on considered answers to correctly understood questions. While considering this issue it is worthwhile to note that occasionally an informant may actually lie. In general, lying on the part of a research informant is thought to be rare in that this type of behaviour on the part of the informant can often be discovered through normal research triangulation procedures. It is well accepted that an informant will have an agenda and that this will result in his or her putting a 'spin' on the data supplied. There is also the fact that the researcher will be on the lookout for information which does not resonate well with his or her understanding of the situation and even this may detect any lies being told.

Even when the informant has understood the question and has been prepared to offer an unambiguous answer, there is no guarantee that the researcher will have understood this answer in the way that the informant intended it to be understood. Individuals sometimes have poor listening skills.

It is essential that the researcher be vigilant and on his or her guard for the possible problems which can arise from such a situation. Berman (2006) [52] provides a comprehensive overview of the issues related to Active Listening in a YouTube presentation.

Despite these problems, interviewing is still one of the most important ways of collecting qualitative data in academic research. The challenges are certainly considerable but it is possible to overcome

---

[52] http://www.youtube.com/watch?v=7AxNI3PhvBo&feature=related

them by the researcher being appropriately aware and prepared to check his or her understanding as they go along.

It is sound research practice for the researcher to provide a copy of the transcript of the interview to the informant with an invitation to the informant to read it and to advise if any misunderstandings have crept into the researcher's record of the interview. Of course, there is some risk involved here in that the informant when he or she reads what has been said could change his or her mind and either make material changes to this transcript or withdraw from the research project completely. Ethics protocols require researchers to alert informants to their right to withdraw from a research project and to have any data they may have supplied removed from the study.

Checking for understanding is not the same as probing or prompting the informant. Probing and prompting the informant can be seen as trying to either acquire more information which the informant does not appear to want to offer or trying to lead the informant's thinking and his or her answers in a particular way. This is not the same as a 'talk tango' and probing and prompting should be used sparingly and with considerable caution.

Being aware of the challenges in understanding informants and recording the data they supply is the first step in being a skilled academic researcher and this note may be of some help in engaging in this issue.

Appendix 5: A short note on two limitations of questionnaires

Questionnaires are a common way of collecting data in social science research. Perhaps not used as frequently as interviews in some academic circles, they are nonetheless an important measuring instrument in the tool kit of the academic researcher.

There are two issues related to the use of questionnaires of which the researcher should be aware. The first of these relates to the egalitarian nature of the data produced in the hands of the researcher. Completed questionnaires are entered once and only once into the data set to be analysed. This is irrespective of who has supplied the data. Therefore the reply of a highly informed respondent is given the same weight as that of a relatively novice or inexperienced one. It is not easy to apply weights to a questionnaire in a convincing manner depending on who completed them (which could be anonymous) and thus all questionnaire responses are invariably equal[53]. If there is a major variance in the experience of potential informants and there is an adequate group of experienced and not so experienced informants, then the researcher should consider conducting two (or more) different surveys. A comparison of these groups could be enlightening and useful.

The second issue is related to the inflexibility associated with the use of a questionnaire as a data collection instrument and process. Having developed a questionnaire, including design (pre-testing and field-testing etc), the researcher attempts to collect as many completed ones as possible. Despite the care taken during the development process there may still be mistakes and challenges in the questionnaire. When the required number of completed question-

[53] Some researchers argue that it is not rational to combine the opinions of experts with the opinions of those who are not so well informed by the use of responses to a questionnaire. Others however, suggest that the principle of the Wisdom of Crowds and an average of the responses will produce a better understanding of the issue.

naires is returned, the researcher commences the process of data capture, analysis and interpretations. At this stage it may become apparent that there is/are one or more poor questions and that no useful data has been obtained from these questions. It is now too late to do anything about this.

Contrast this to the process of obtaining research data using an interview schedule during an interview. An interview schedule like a questionnaire will have been designed, pre-tested and field-tested etc. but despite the care taken by this there may still be poorly worded questions in the interview schedule. If this is the case the problem will almost certainly make itself apparent during the first interview and the problem with the poor question/s can be addressed immediately. This flexibility is important to academic researchers.

Some researchers find the idea of this level of flexibility unsettling especially if the problem with the interview schedule if discovered after a number of interviews have been completed. How can data be compared in a consistent manner if the interview schedule has been changed? It is possible that the data might be incommensurable and if this is the case, care needs to be taken with the analysis. Any changes to the interview schedule during the research will need to be specifically reported in dissertation. Whatever the challenges it is better to improve a poorly worded question when it is discovered in the interview schedule than to continue with it.

The two issues discussed above do not invalidate the use of questionnaires in academic research. However, it is important that academic researchers are aware of these issues.

Appendix 6: A short note on samples and saturation in qualitative research provided by Dr K Grant

When planning fieldwork, researchers in general and doctoral candidates in particular have to make decisions on how and from whom to collect their data. For those following a positivist paradigm and using quantitative techniques there is abundant guidance, with a solid statistical foundation using probability sampling of a target population. However, others, particularly those adopting phenomenological perspectives, make extensive use of qualitative techniques, including interviews, case studies, observation and action research. In these situations the sampling method used is *purposive* or *non-probability* sampling, where "the subjective judgments of the researcher are used in selecting the sample" (Remenyi et al., 1998).

Purposive Sampling Approaches

Purposive sampling is a widely used technique in social science research. In purposive sampling, cases/participants are selected to meet a specific set of criteria. Examples include choosing convenient, typical or modal respondents, heterogeneous or diverse respondents, experts, extreme/critical/exemplar cases and snowball selection (where initial participants point the researcher to others).

Purposive sampling uses "information rich cases…from which one can learn a great deal about central issues of great importance to the purpose of the research" (Patton, 2002:46).

Some authors, for example Coyne (1997), differentiate between purposive and *theoretical* sampling, drawing on the work of Strauss and Corbin (1990), where theoretical sampling in grounded theory means "sampling on the basis of concepts that have proven theoretical relevance to the evolving theory'".

Sample Size

Most texts on qualitative research are silent on sample size. As Guest et al concluded from a review of twenty-four research methods books and seven databases, the "literature did a poor job of operationalizing the concept of saturation, providing no description of how saturation might be determined and no practical guidelines for estimating sample sizes for purposively sampled interviews" (Guest et al., 2006:60). As an example, in one widely used reference text, Patton commented: "There are no rules for sample size in qualitative enquiry. Sample size depends on what you want to know, the purpose of the inquiry, what's at stake, what will be useful, what will have credibility and what can be done with available time and resources." (Patton, 2002:244)

Some limited guidance for specific sample sizes is available. Table 1 summarises recommendations made for several types of study.

Author	Recommendation
Bernard (2000:178)	Most ethnographic studies are based on 30-60 interviews
Bertaux (1981)	The smallest acceptable sample size in qualitative research is 15.
Morse (1994:225)	At least 6 participants for phenomenological studies; approximately 30-50 participants for ethnographies, grounded theory studies, and ethnoscience studies
Creswell (1998)	Between 5 and 25 interviews for a phenomenological study and 20-30 for a grounded theory study.
Kuzel (1992:41)	6 to 8 interviews for a homogeneous sample and 12-20 data sources "when looking for disconfirming evidence or trying to achieve maximum variation."
Sandelowski (1995:182)	A phenomenological study "will likely require 10 to 50 descriptions of a target experience in order to discern its necessary and sufficient constituents"

Table1: Recommendations for Sample Size in Purposive Sampling

Saturation

Determining saturation seems to be a decision for the individual researcher. However Guest et al suggest that "theoretical saturation relates to the development of theory" and such saturation might be held to have occurred when "new information produces little or no change to the code book" (Guest et al., 2006:65). They then describe "thematic prevalence" where they define "the importance of a code as the proportion of individual interviews to which a code is applied" and suggest testing for consistency in theme responses as a method of determining data saturation.

In most discussions on sampling, the unit of analysis might be an individual or an organisation and either might be referred to as a "case". Patton (2002:448) describes multiple layers of cases and Yin identifies four types of case study (Yin, 2003:40).

Gummesson (2000:95), drawing on the work of Glaser and Strauss (1967), argue that "theories and models that purport to have a degree of generality" can be based on a limited number of cases, with saturation being "the diminishing marginal contribution of each additional case". Yin, in discussing multiple case studies, suggests that the selection of cases be done using "replication, not sampling logic". Replication can be literal (predicting similar results) or theoretical (expected differences but for predictable reasons) (Yin, 2003:47-48). Yin also describes a framework for multiple case studies which examines the results from each successive replication to determine whether any changes to theory or protocol are needed (a form of saturation testing), concluding that anywhere from two or three to as many as five or six replications depending on the degree of difference between cases (ibid:50-51).

Saturation Examples

To conclude, Table 2 provides examples of studies demonstrating saturation, which include explicit discussion of how saturation was determined.

Author	Findings
Romney et al (1986:326)	In situations of "cultural competence" (i.e. well informed individuals in a homogeneous culture) as few as 4 respondents can produce a high level of accuracy and that well below 30 is a reliable sample.
Marshall (1996:524)	In a purposive sample of physicians, thematic saturation was evident after about 15 interviews and theoretical saturation occurred after 24 interviews
Guest et al (2006:78)	In examining a sample of 60 interviews, found that "data saturation had for the most part occurred by the time we had analyzed 12 interviews". In further examining how many interviews were necessary to have supported the four themes they developed in their study they found that "enough data existed after 6 interviews to support these four themes". They concluded that, "For most research enterprises, however, in which the aim is to understand common perceptions and experiences among a group of relatively homogeneous individuals, 12 interviews should suffice".
Mason (2010)	Examined 563 PhDs that used qualitative approaches and found, in the 179 examples that followed a case study approach, between 1 and 95 interviews were carried out, with a median of 33 interviews.
Bruggeman, (2010)	Reached saturation at about 25 interviews (of some 40 carried out)

Table2: Specific Examples of Purposive Sampling

References

Bernard, h. R. (2000) *social research methods,* thousand oaks, ca, sage.

Bertaux, d. (1981) from the life-history approach to the transformation of sociological practice. In bertaux, d. (ed.) *Biography and society: the life history approach in the social sciences.* London, sage.

Bruggeman, s. (2010) a knowledge integration perspective on the study of self-initiated expatriates. *Henley business school.* Unversity of reading.

Coyne, i. T. (1997) sampling in qualitative research. Purposeful and theoretical sampling; merging or clear boundaries? *Journal of advanced nursing,* 26.

Creswell, j. (1998) *qualitative inquiry and research design: choosing among five traditions,* thousand oaks, ca, sage.

Glaser, b. G. & strauss, a. L. (1967) *the discovery of grounded theory,* new york, aldine.

Guest, g., bunce, a. & johnson, l. (2006) how many interviews are enough? An experiment with data saturation and variability. *Field methods,* 18**,** 59.

Gummesson, e. (2000) *qualitative methods in management research, second edition,* thousand oaks, ca, sage publications.

Kuzel, a. (1992) sampling in qualitative inquiry. In crabtree, b. & miller, w. (eds.) *Doing qualitative research.* Newbury park, ca, sage.

Marshall, m. N. (1996) sampling for qualitative research. *Family practice,* 13.

Mason, m. (2010) sample size and saturation in phd studies using qualitative interviews. *Forum qualitative sozialforschung / forum: qualitative social research,* 11.

Morse, j. (1994) designing funded qualitative research. In denzin, n. & lincoln, y. (eds.) *Handbook for qualitative research.* Thousand oaks, ca, sage.

Patton, m. (2002) *qualitative research and evaluation methods. 3rd ed,* thousand oaks, ca, sage.

Romney, a. K., batchelder, s. C. & weller, w. H. (1986) culture as consensus: a theory of culture and informant accuracy. *American anthropologist* 88**,** 313–38.

Sandelowski, m. (1995) sample size in qualitative research. *Research in nursing & health,* 18.

Yin, r. K. (2003) *case study research: design and methods., third edition,* thousand oaks, california, sage publications.

Appendix 7: Observation as supplementary and contextual data to interviews

Observation is regarded as the central platform on which research designs such as participant-observer works as well as on which action research and ethnographic studies are based. However there are also opportunities for observation to play an important supplementary role in both interviews and focus groups. The researcher's observations related to informants and their organisation can be critical in understanding the context of the research, which is essential in business and management studies. In this Appendix observation in this latter sense is discussed.

With regards to academic interviews and focus groups observation refers to data acquired that is not obtained as a direct response to a question asked by a researcher. Observation may be what is seen, heard, smelt, tasted or felt by the researcher. The researcher receives this type of data continually during interviews, but it is not uncommon for the researcher who is busy relating to the informant's spoken data or focus group's discussion to not be consciously aware of this observation data and thus it may be disregarded and lost. Observation based data is generally less formal than the data acquired though an interview or a focus group. Except in special circumstances, observations are not immediately recorded and the delay in reducing them to writing can produce challenges. Observation data which is properly recorded can be a useful source of understanding and should be regarded as a potential source of important data, even when it is supplementary data to interviews and thus in the normal course of events not regarded perhaps as being more important than the data acquired during the interview. Observation is also a useful source of data from a triangulation point of view.

All data collection has to be grounded in a continuous awareness of the research question and the sub-questions. It is critical that this focus is maintained through the entire research process. Data which does not contribute to answering or at least increasing the researcher's understanding of the research question is not data at all, but rather *noise* and should be largely ignored. During the early part of the research process it is not always immediately obvious whether something is noise or data but the researcher will acquire skill at determining this as he or she proceeds with the research. If the researcher discovers that much of what has been collected as data does not make the requisite contribution to answering the research question then this activity of collecting irrelevant material will have to be abandoned.

Observation is sometimes described as being either covert or overt. Covert observation takes place when the individuals being observed are not aware of the fact that this is happening. This type of research involves deliberately misleading the research participants. Academic research generally does not approve of such research, although exceptions can be made in circumstances where there will be no question of the research participants coming to any direct or indirect harm by the research study. It can be difficult to have an ethics protocol approved if covert observation is involved. Observation is said to be overt when the individuals being observed are aware of their being a part of a research study. Such awareness can have a direct affect on the behaviour of the research participants. A classic example of overt observation is the research conducted at the Hawthorn Plant of the GE Company in 1923. At the General Electric Plant researchers increased levels of lighting and observed increases in worker productivity as the levels of lighting improved. It is probably the best known instance of an overt observation research project in business and management studies that directly affected the performance of the research participants.

Using observation as supplementary data to support interviews is not easily categorised as either covert or overt observation. It is not covert as there is no attempt to hide the fact that the researcher can observe his or her surroundings and what is happening during the data collection process. It also should be understood by all concerned that the opinions of the researcher will be influenced by that which is observed. On the other hand as overt observation is normally conducted as part of a formal experimental type intervention, observation used as support data for the research project, it is often not directly referred to by the researcher or mentioned in the Letter of Consent.

Observations normally begin with subjective impressions the researcher receives from contact with a potential informant or a potential informant's organisation. Subjective impressions on their own do not generally constitute useful data. However subjective impressions on which the researcher reflects can constitute useful insights, which may either open up new lines of enquiry or may lead to confirmation of analysis that has been conducted using other data and thus is a form of triangulation. From this it may be seen that there are three steps involved in using observation data which are:

1. register the observation with as little bias as possible;
2. record it as soon as possible in order to minimise recall issues;
3. reflect on what meaning may be abstracted from the observations.

Field notes can be used to record the observations. These should be comprehensive but also parsimonious. It can be tempting for the researcher to produce too much unwanted data. These field notes will be transformed into a narrative similar to that discussed below. Then it is a question of the personal reflections of the researcher. Reflection has always been an important part of academic research. However today research degree candidates are expected to not only reflect on their work as they proceed through the research process, but also to comment on their reflections and to report on how these thoughts have influenced them. It is worth pointing out that some researchers fall into the trap of spending too much time reflecting and this can slow down or interrupt the research process.

Observing and recording data does not directly explain behaviour and it may not useful to impute motive to the behaviour observed at too early a stage. There needs to be a dialectic type involvement between the observations and the other data acquired through the interview process. This dialectic type process requires the researcher to reflect on what could be the meaning of the behaviours observed. It is important to remember that these observations need to be contextualised in the requirement to help answer or understand the research question. By and large the researcher will find a mix of behaviours, some of which will not be consistent with what informants will have been saying. In some research studies there are sometimes disconnects between what the researcher is told and what actually happens. Observation can make the researcher more sensitive to possible contradictions in the organisation and thus alert him or herself to any disconnects and can provide a guide to additional areas which may be fruitful to explore.

Data available from observation begins with the first contact with the informant or the informant's organisation. This first contact may be by telephone, by e-mail or it could be by personal introduction at a meeting. Whichever approach was used to make contact it is unlikely that any formal data would be collected, but there will be opportunities for observations. The following is an example of a chain of events leading to the commencement of a case study research project in a large global organisation. The research question is *How does an organisation cope with the speed of response issue when in a highly competitive market which is driven by new technological innovation?*

> *The first contact was made by the researcher telephoning the organisation and asking to speak to the Chief Executive Officer (CEO). Having been connected to the CEO's Personal Assistant (PA) the researcher was asked to write in and request access to the organisation for his research. He was also asked to supply a letter from the business school to con-*

firm his status as a researcher. These requirements were duly complied with. A prompt reply was received from the organisation to the fact that the papers arrived and that they would be attended to in the following weeks.

The researcher then continued to seek other case study participants as he required about four different organisations for his study.

The weeks went by during which another large national organisation was recruited as a case study participant. After about eight weeks and just before the researcher was about to make contact with the global organisation to enquire about the progress of his request he received a letter from the CEO's PA to the effect that the organisation would cooperate with his research. He was told the board of directors had agreed to this. A competent gatekeeper had been appointed by the organisation to assist the researcher in finding appropriate people to interview and to assist in obtaining other data he might acquire.

The gatekeeper was based in an office at a site which was nearly an hour's train journey or an hour and a half drive away in an industrial park. He was a middle to senior ranking executive. The organisation's site was a relatively modern looking multi-story glass building. It had a controlled parking area which required an invitation before obtaining access. On entering the building there was a reception desk and a seating area. The receptionist advises that the gatekeeper will arrive within 10 minutes to collect the researcher. The researcher is asked to complete a visitor's register and is give a temporary security clearance badge.

The gatekeeper arrived promptly. He is wearing a formal gray pinstripe suit with white shirt and dark tie. He has his security badge displayed over his breast pocket. The gatekeeper introduces himself using his surname only. The researcher obtains the impression that he is a formal person who would not be interested to be on a first name basis.

The gatekeeper's office was on the 10th floor in a panelled off section of an open plan office which accommodated market planning analysts. The office was sparsely furnished. There was an air of formality about this work place layout. There was no secretarial assistance. On the way to the office the gatekeeper offered the researcher a cup of coffee which was acquired from a vending machine.

The gatekeeper explains that the researcher has to use the gatekeeper to make all contacts with employees and all requests for information or data. It is clear that the gatekeeper wants to have a direct say in the course of the research.

Over the next few months 12 interviews are arranged with executives. They are all polite and they answer the question put to them with authority. They divert their telephones for the duration of the interview. They supply supporting data when requested, but the researcher is asked not to make copies of these documents and to return them when he is finished with them.

The informants were generally middle aged with more than 20 years experience with the organisation.

There is a degree of similarity in the buildings and the offices used by these people. They all comply with the company dress code. The politeness afforded to the researcher is excellent except that a few people are unable to commence the interview at the appointed time. One executive is two hours late and the researcher has to sit in the waiting room for this period. It appears that these executives are under pressure.

When the 12 interviews have been transcribed and the case study written up the researcher offered a copy of the case study report to the gatekeeper so that he could circulate it to the informants to check in order to ensure that the researcher had understood the material he obtained correctly and that the case study report reflected the situation. It took the organisation three months to respond and no changes were required and except for a request that no one be named in the case study there were no restrictions placed on the case study.

Reflecting on the above narrative it appears that the organisation shows evidence of it being a formal and bureaucratic establishment. There is control of access to buildings, to parking and to refreshments. The gatekeeper will have control over who the researcher will interview and the informants, although they will give opinions relatively freely do not want any of the documents which they are prepared to show the researcher to fall outside of their control. There is evidence that the organisation is not fast moving at either the strategic or the tactical level.

Looking at the above observation data alone is of course only part of the story. The research question addressed the issue of organisational change and how organisations need to respond to technology developments, which might afford them competitive advantage. One of the key characteristics of organisations who use this type of technology development is that they are highly flexible. High flexibility is not often associated with bureaucratic establishments. Although the interviewed informants claimed that they possessed a flexible outlook and were able to quickly respond to changes in the marketplace the apparent culture of the organisation was not congruent with such assertions. There appears to be a disconnect between what the researcher hears and what he observes.

Reflecting on the disconnect between the data supplied by the informants and the observations obtained by the researcher is an important issue. This might prompt the researcher to explore these issues further. On the other hand the research agenda may not allow the time or the space to do this.

If the researcher decides to proceed with the data collected so far, the disconnect between the data sources needs explanation. It would not be appropriate in an academic research project to leave such a situation dangling and thus he needs to find a possible explanation.

One suggestion might be that the degree of flexibility claimed by the informants within an organisation is a reflection of the internal sense of flexibility. The employees interviewed all had long periods of service. They may not have experiences of any other organisation in a position of an executive. They believed that they were flexible and fast moving largely because they have no other experience with which to compare how they behaved. This is of course only one possible explanation and it is not suggested that it is the only one. The point is that the supplementary data collected through the process of observation gave the researcher another lens with which to view the organisation and provided an opportunity to authenticate the informants' data or evidence. It would be unfortunate if the researcher had not been sensitised to observation data and how it may be used.

As a final point of reflection the reader should note that there are other interpretations of the apparent disconnect between the data described above.

Glossary of Terms

Academic research
The process of adding something of value to the body of theoretic knowledge by answering a research question or questions. In addition an important characteristic of academic research is that it needs to be presented in such a way to demonstrate a high degree of scholarship on the part of the researcher.

Alternative hypothesis
Hypothesis testing attempts to reject a claim which is made by the researcher. This claim is called the Null Hypothesis. If this claim is rejected then the Alternative Hypothesis which needs to be stated at the same time as the Null Hypothesis is accepted (pro tem).

Application for research ethics approval
The procedure for acquiring ethics approval is to complete an application form and to attach to it the documents which are appropriate to the research project. These documents are then presented to the Research Ethics Committee (REC). The number and specific documents which need to be submitted will vary according to the project but will generally include a proposed Letter of Informed Consent, a Research Participants Information Sheet/s, a Proposed Letter of Approval from any other interested body such as a Professional Society of which the researcher/s is/are members etc. The application form is signed by the lead researcher. Research ethics approval needs to be acquired before the research can commence.

Balanced question
A question or item in a questionnaire with a scale that offers an equal number of positive scoring possibilities and negative scoring possibilities.

Bespoke questionnaire
A questionnaire designed by the researcher himself or herself for specific use in the research being undertaken. It is to be contrasted

with an off-the-shelf questionnaire which has been previously used and validated elsewhere.

Bias

From a research point of view bias refers to the introduction of a non-random element in the choices made by the researcher. From a statistical point of view bias refers to systematic error which could be due to choice of sample, measurement technique or some other element of research design. Bias may also be introduced during the analysis, interpretation and conclusion phases of the research. A bias may be the result of a preconception of the characteristics of a person, a situation or an organisation, to mention only three such issues. It can be difficult for a researcher to be aware of his/her biases.

Body language

Researchers should when conducting an interview take into account how the informant is sitting and physically reacting to the questions being asked. This reading of body language can give the researcher clues as to how reliable the data obtained from the interview might be.

Conclusions

Research findings on their own alone will generally not provide the degree of insights sought. Thus the researcher needs to summarise the findings and to state what they mean to his/her community. This part of the research is referred to as writing or producing the conclusions.

Correspondence analysis

Correspondence analysis is sometimes described as an extension of content analysis as it requires data similar to content analysis. However correspondence analysis requires the creation of a 2 by 2 matrix which records the major concepts or issues discussed. It also reflects who mentioned which concepts or issues. With this matrix it is possible to produce a number of reports which show the association of the concepts or issues and the different groups which held these views. Note the word Correspondence is a French word meaning association or connection.

Data
Data are numbers, words, or images or sounds or other sensory stimuli which causes a researcher to take notice and which he or she may or will use in his or her research process. Data needs to be contrasted with information which is sometimes referred to as data which has been processed or structured.

Debate
The purpose of a focus group is not to collect primary data about the issues being researched, but rather to obtain insights into the research topic by listening to knowledgeable informants debate or discuss important issues related to the research question. This is sometimes referred to as a discourse.

Debriefing
In the context of academic research debriefing is the process of describing what has transpired during a research encounter.

Delphi study
A questionnaire based study which requires the collaboration of a group of experts and a 3-round questionnaire process. A Delphi Study questionnaire is included in the examples provided in this book.

Descriptive statistics
The use of measures of central tendency and dispersion together with relevant tables and graphs in order to describe a population.

Discourse
See debate above.

Duration of a focus group
The time required to conduct a focus group. A focus group should not take more than 90 minutes as any period in excess of this will be tiring to the individuals involved and may thus produce poor results.

Ethics protocol
The identification of any potential ethical issues related to the research process together with the way in which this potential ethical problem will be avoided or ameliorated constitutes the protocol. The ethics protocol is usually written by the research candidate and approved by an ethics committee. Data collection should not begin until the ethics protocol has been approved.

Evidence
The word evidence may be used as a synonym for data. Some academic researchers prefer the word evidence as it does not have the same connotation of authority as data and this is considered more appropriate for doctoral research.

Existing questionnaires
A researcher can either develop his or her own questionnaire or used an already made one. A self developed questionnaire which is sometimes described as a bespoke questionnaire requires a considerable amount of development work including pre- and field testing. A pre-existing questionnaire which has been previously validated may be used with less preliminary work.

Expletives
In the context of academic research an expletive is a word which would not in the normal course of events be acceptable in polite company. Many of these words are four letters and would also be called "bad language".

Face-to-face interview
There are several types of interviews. These include face-to-face interviewing where the informant and the researcher meet in close proximity. Telephone and internet interviewing where the informant and the researcher do not meet are also sometimes used.

Facilitator (focus group)
An individual who works with a focus group to ensure that all the members have an equal chance to express themselves and their views during the meeting. Sometimes referred to as a moderator

this individual will also ensure that the discussion stays on track and that a suitable record is taken of the discussion. The facilitator may also be responsible for obtaining the Letters of Consent etc. Facilitating or moderating a focus group is a skill which needs to be learnt by the researcher.

Field diary
See field note.

Field note
The creation of a written note by the researcher made during or immediately after an encounter with an informant or a research situation. Field notes are sometimes collected in a field diary.

Field procedures
The set of activities required to collect data or evidence from informants. These activities range from making appointments to understanding the dress code to having a device to record interviews if appropriate.

Field studies
Research conducted outside of the library or the laboratory in a natural setting.

Field test
Before using a questionnaire or an interview schedule it is useful to test it on a small number of respondents. This is sometimes also referred to as a pilot test. Any questions which are not clear or any words that are unfamiliar to the test participants should be changed or removed.

Findings
The results of the analysis of the data collected and/or the synthesis of the ideas used in a theoretical research project.

Focus group
A meeting of a number of knowledgeable informants who have come together to discuss and debate a number of questions put to

them by a researcher for the purpose of clarifying issues related to the research question.

Forced question
A question in a questionnaire which does not provide an option of being neutral or undecided.

Gatekeeper
A gatekeeper is a person who can either facilitate or can obstruct a researcher when he or she is trying to find appropriate knowledgeable informants. The gatekeeper could be a personal assistant or it could be an associate of the person with which the researcher may want to make contact. Sometimes a gatekeeper can be an organisation such as a professional institute. For example if the research obtains endorsement from the Institute of Bankers for the research project then it will usually be easy to obtain the support of individual banks.

Granularity of the scale
The number of possible options available across a scale. A scale of 1 to 10 has a higher degree of granularity than a 1 to 5 scale.

Hypothesis
A claim articulated by a researcher for the purposes of determining whether the claim can be rejected by statistical techniques.

Hypothesis testing
The way in which researchers attempt to refute an hypothesis. An hypothesis test will involve a Null Hypothesis and an Alternative Hypothesis. If the Null Hypothesis is rejected then the Alternative Hypothesis is accepted.

Inferential statistics
Statistical techniques which may be used in order to generalise from a sample to a population.

Internet questionnaire
A questionnaire which is distributed to potential informants by means of the internet, the most usual form of which has been e-mail.

Inter-organisational focus groups
Focus groups which are composed of members from different organisations

Interpretive research
This term is usually used to describe a research approach which does not rely on the use of standard mathematical modelling or inferential statistical techniques.

Interview
The process of formally obtaining verbal data from an informant.

Intra-organisational focus groups
Focus groups which are composed of members from within the same organisation.

Multi-person interviewing
Some researchers attempt to interview more than one informant at a time. The result of this technique is often that the data is not as rich as it would have been if the interviews had been carried out on a one-to-one basis. Focus groups are sometimes mistakenly referred to as multiple interviews.

Knowledgeable informant
An individual who has the data or has access to the data required by the researcher to help answer the research question.

Likert type scale
A scale used in a questionnaire which has the same form as that used by Likert in his original paper. The term likert type is used because some researchers believe that in order to refer to a scale as Likert it should be a 1 to 5 and not 1 to 7 or 1 to 9 which are also commonly used.

Moderator
See Facilitator.

Naturally occurring data
Data which already exists before the research has commenced such as financial reports or correspondence between individuals is sometimes referred to as naturally occurring data and is contrasted with researcher provoked data which is produced during interviews, focus groups or questionnaires.

Observation
Observation usually refers to the collecting of data by visual means including inspection. Arriving at the premises of an informant may give a researcher a number of important data point to include in the research transcript.

Postal questionnaire
A questionnaire which is despatched to a potential informant by means of the postal services.

Protocol
A list of issues and requirements to ensure that a research technique is rigorously executed.

Pre-existing groups
When seeking to use a focus group technique the researcher may invite individuals to come together for the first time or the researcher may request a pre-existing group such as a committee which is already established to act as a focus group for the research.

Pre-testing
Before a field test can be conducted the researcher should undertake some pre-testing with colleagues and associates or friends.

Proposition
This term is used in qualitative research instead of hypothesis. Propositions are tested in qualitative research. However the method of using a Null Hypothesis and an Alternative Hypothesis

which underpins quantitative research is not associated with testing a proposition which is less formal.

Qualitative questionnaire
Questionnaires where the majority of the questions are open ended and thus require explanations from the informant. Such a questionnaire may also have questions requiring nominal or categorical data replies.

Qualitative research
Research which follows the same framework as interpretivist research described above. Some researchers argue that the terms qualitative and interpretivist research are problematic. It is argued that research is the same regardless of whether the data is qualitative or quantitative. This view is not universally accepted.

Quantitative research
Research which employs mathematical and statistical techniques.

Mixed methods
An approach to research which employs both quantitative and qualitative approaches

Pilot study
This is another term for a field test. The pilot study is essential and it should be carried out involving individuals who are or who could be informants for the main study to follow. Researchers need to listen carefully to the critique they receive during the pilot or field test.

Purposeful sample
A sample which is not a random sample. Therefore a purposeful sample could be a convenience sample or a snowball sample etc. The elements in a purposeful sample are selected for a specific reason by the researcher. For example, conducting a survey of smokers requires a purposeful sample.

Random sample
A sample where all the informants have had an equal probability of being chosen.

Reflection

Reflection has become an important part of academic research. Reflection requires a process of inward examination by the researcher to see if he or she can find any further understanding of the research. Reflection has been referred to as "Active, persistent, and careful consideration of any belief or supposed form of knowledge in the light of the grounds that support it, and the further conclusions to which it tends, constitutes reflective thought". *Dewey J, 1991, How we think, Prometheus Books, p6, NY*

Refusal to sign

Refusal to sign occurs when an informant is not prepared to sign the Letter of Informed Consent.

Research Ethics committee

Universities and other research institutions have appointed a group of individuals who are charged with scrutinising applications for ethics approval before they are permitted to commence their research. There are normally a number of different levels of research ethics committees ranging from the highest level in the University which is a Senate sub-committee to Faculty Ethics Committees to School or Department Ethics Committees. Where the number of students is large research Ethics Approval is sometimes delegated to the researchers' supervisors.

Research question

One of the fundamental characteristics of research in business and management studies is that it normally should attempt to answer a specific question. The research question is usually seen as the fulcrum about which other research methodology decisions are centred. There is often one primary or main research question which can be reduced or unpacked to several more detailed sub-questions.

Research Sub-questions

Detailed questions which have been identified as needing answering so that the primary or main research question many be answered.

The establishment of sub-questions is as important as developing an interview schedule or a questionnaire.

Researcher provoked data
See naturally occurring data.

Rules of the focus group meeting
Members of a focus group need to comply with the rules of the meeting which contain issues such as only one person may speak at a time and no one should make any belittling comment about another person's point of view.

Sample
A sub-set of the population which the researcher is studying.

Self selection
Self selection occurs when individuals offer themselves as informants to be interviewed or join a focus group or complete a questionnaire. Individuals who volunteer in this way may have an agenda and this may introduce a bias into the data.

ServQual
An approach to questionnaire development where a set of questions are asked of an informant twice. The first set is to establish the informants' expectations and the second set is to gauge the informants' experience. This is related to an enquiry of service levels. An example of such a questionnaire is provided in this book.

Snowball sample
A snowball sample is one which is developed by the researcher through introductions from successful informants. After contact with an informant the researcher requests information from the informant as to who might also be prepared to supply the researcher with appropriate data. In this way a sample of informants is developed.

Sub-questions
Research questions are often difficult to answer as one issue. Sometimes it is necessary to create sub-questions which when answered will facilitate the answering of the main research question.

Survey
A survey is a detailed and formal examination of a subject or a person or an organisation etc. The word survey is used in research in two ways. Firstly there is a large scale survey which refers to the use of some sort of questionnaire administered to a large number of potential informants. The second use of the word is as an in-depth survey and that refers to interviewing informants to acquire a larger amount of data than can be produced by a questionnaire.

Testable propositions
Research requires questions to be answered and this is sometimes done by stating propositions which are tested and the result of the test helps answer the research question. When a qualitative or interpretivist approach to the research is taken the issues being tested are referred to as a proposition. When quantitative research is employed the term hypothesis is usually used instead of proposition.

Transcription
Creating a formal written statement which includes the questions put to an informant and the replies received.

Virtual focus groups
It is sometimes suggested that a focus group could be conducted over the internet using teleconferencing software. If a video conference was held then it would be possible to obtain some of the richness which can be obtained from a focus discussion.

Web based questionnaires
A questionnaire which is placed on a website. Informants are invited to visit the website and complete the questionnaire.

Wisdom of Crowds

The Wisdom of Crowds is an expression/concept used to indicate that sometimes the average value of a variable estimated by a diverse group of people may produce a satisfactory result.

Index